# the great lobster

## and crab cookbook

whitecap

First published by: R&R Publications Marketing Pty. Ltd.
ACN 27 062 090 555
12 Edward Street, Brunswick Victoria 3056 Australia
©Richard Carroll

This edition published in 2004 in the U.S. and Canada by Whitecap Books Ltd.
For more information, contact:
Whitecap Books
351 Lynn Avenue
North Vancouver
British Columbia
Canada V7J 2C4

©Richard Carroll


Publisher: Richard Carroll
Production Manager: Anthony Carroll
Designer: Vincent Wee
Creative Director: Paul Sims
Computer Graphics: Lucy Adams
Food Photography: Gary Smith
Food Stylist: Janet Lodge
Food for Photography: Louise Hockham and Katrina Cleary
Recipe Development: Ellen Argyriou, Janet Lodge and Lyn Carroll
Proof Reader: Fiona Brodribb
Editor of North American Edition: Marial Shea

The publishers would like to thank the management and staff of the Prince Edward Island Department of Fisheries and Aquaculture, especially Mr. Parnell Trainor,
for their assistance in providing information and recipes pertaining to the Northern Lobster.

National Library of Canada Cataloguing in Publication Data

Main entry under title:
The great lobster and crab cookbook / editor, Marial Shea ; recipe development, Ellen Argyriou ... [et al.]. -- North American ed.

(Great seafood series)
Includes bibliographical references and index.
ISBN 1-55285-536-8
1. Cookery (Lobsters)  2. Cookery (Crabs)  I. Argyriou, Ellen. II. Shea, Marial.  III. Series.
TX754.L63G73 2003      641.6'95      C2003-911234-9

First Edition Printed August 2002
Computer Typeset in Verdana, Trojan and Charcoal


Printed in Indonesia

The publisher acknowledges the financial support of the Government of Canada through the Book
Publishing Industry Development Program for our publishing activities.

# contents

# INTRODUCTION

Sink your teeth into our succulent crab and lobster dishes. We have gathered together recipes that elicit the best flavors from these fabulous foods from the sea. From soups that flood your house with blissful aromas to main meals that are bursting with color in a celebration of the world's most treasured cuisines, you are bound to enjoy every mouthful.

We have provided signposts on your journey, with expert advice on how to prepare, cook, clean and store crab and lobster to attain the most tender, mouth-watering tastes. A few secrets revealed will mean you can determine whether your seafood is fresh, and other tips will ensure that your results match those found in even the finest, silver-service restaurants. So prepare yourself for the gustatory delights of the deep.

# CRAB PREPARATION

## To Buy

Do not buy or cook dead blue crabs. You can buy blue crabs either raw or cooked in the shell.

Under no circumstances should live blue crabs and cooked blue crabs touch each other. Live crabs may contain bacteria that could contaminate the cooked crab.

## To Store

Wrap the crab in plastic wrap or foil or store in an airtight container in the refrigerator for up to 3 days or you can freeze up to 3 months providing your freezer operates at 0°F/-18°C.

## To Cook

The most humane method to prepare live crab is to place the crab into the freezer for several hours. This method does not freeze the meat but has an anaesthetizing effect on the crab. (Never plunge into boiling water as this toughens the meat and the claws can fall off. It is also generally thought to be more painful for the crab.)

Alternatively, to kill the crab instantly, stab it just behind the eyes with the point of a sharp knife (step 1). Place the crab into cold water, cover the pan and bring to boil. Simmer 5–20 minutes (depending upon size). The crab is cooked when it turns a bright orange color.

## To Clean

Place the crab on its back, and gently fold back the tail flap or apron. Twist and pull the apron off. You will find that the intestinal vein is attached and will pull out along the apron. Discard (step 2).

Hold the crab with one hand where the apron was removed. Use the other hand to pry up, tear off and discard the top shell. Remove the gills, take out the greyish bag and pull out mandibles from the front of the crab (step 3).

Hold the body where the legs were attached and apply pressure so that the crab splits in half along the center of the body. Fold back the halves and twist apart (step 4).

Twist off the claws and legs where they join the body. Crack with a hammer or nutcracker to make the meat easy to remove.

*Step 1*

*Step 2*

*Step 3*

*Step 4*

# LOBSTER PREPARATION

## To Buy

Lobsters may be purchased live, or freshly cooked, in the shell. For both live and cooked, the tail section should spring back into a curled position after being straightened out.

When purchased live, they should show lively movement. Lobsters that show no movement when handled and have a tail that hangs down straight are dead and should be discarded. When handling live lobster, be careful of the claws (if they have any) as they can give you a severe pinch. To protect the handler and to prevent the lobsters from harming each other in captivity, the claws are usually immobilized by placing an elastic band around them.

When buying cooked lobster, check that they are a bright red-orange color and have a fresh aroma.

## To Store

Live lobster should never be placed in fresh water or on ice. Under ideal cool, damp storage conditions, lobster can live out of water for up to 36 hours. They can be stored in your refrigerator for several hours by placing them in a large container covered with damp newspaper or seaweed. Cooked lobster in the shell can be stored in the refrigerator for up to 2 days if placed in a tightly covered container. Shucked lobster meat can be refrigerated for 2–3 days.

Live lobster should never be frozen but cooked lobster freezes well. For best results, the cooked meat should be removed from the shell and placed in plastic containers or freezer bags. Prepare a brine solution of 2oz/50g salt to each 4 cups/ 1 litre of fresh water. Pour this over the lobster so that all the meat is covered and a 1/2in/1cm headspace remains.

Whole cooked lobster can be frozen in individual heavy plastic bags. Place the lobster in the bag, being careful that the sharp shell does not puncture the bag, cover with a brine solution, then cover tightly and freeze. To thaw lobster, place in the refrigerator and allow 18 hours for defrosting. To speed up defrosting time, place the package under cold running water until thawed.

## To Cook

To cook live lobster, the most humane way is to place the lobster in the freezer then simmer it as you would a crab. Lobster should be cooked either in clean sea water or salted fresh water. Lobster will cook in 12–20 minutes depending on size. Drain immediately and serve hot or chill quickly by dipping in cold water.

## To Clean

Hold the lobster right-side-up on a firm surface. Pierce the shell at the center of the body, behind the head (step 1).

Cut the lobster in half lengthwise and remove and discard the sac near the head, and the intestinal vein in the tail. Remove any roe from the body and reserve for flavoring sauces (step 2).

Clean the lobster by rinsing under cold, running water (step 3).

*Step 1*

*Step 2*

*Step 3*

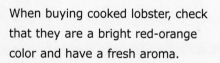

# NUTRITIONAL INFORMATION

**For 3½ oz (100g) serving**

|                           | Crab   | Lobster |
|---------------------------|--------|---------|
| **Protein**               | 19.1g  | 19.4g   |
| **Fat**                   | 0.9g   | 0.8g    |
| **Calories**              | 99     | 98      |
| **Saturated Fat**         | 0.3g   | 0.2g    |
| **Monounsaturated fat**   | 0.2g   | 0.2g    |
| **Total polyunsaturated fat** | 0.4g | 0.4g  |
| **Omega 3s**              | 0.43g  | 0.49g   |
| **Cholesterol**           | 68mg   | 98mg    |

8

# SOUPS & SALADS

SOUPS & SALADS

## Prawn and Crab Soup

### INGREDIENTS

6 tomatoes, chopped

2 onions, chopped

1 tablespoon/15mL vegetable oil

4 cloves garlic, crushed

1 tablespoon/15mL oregano leaves

2 fresh cilantro bunches

1 fish head, such as snapper, perch,
   cod or haddock

10 cups/2.5L water

2 uncooked crabs, cleaned and
   cut into serving pieces

12 medium uncooked prawns (shrimp)
   shelled and deveined

7oz/200g fish fillet, cut into chunks

### METHOD

**1.** Place the tomatoes and onions in a food processor or blender and process to make a purée.

**2.** Heat the oil in a saucepan over medium heat, add the garlic and cook, stirring, for 1 minute or until golden. Stir in the tomato mixture, then add oregano leaves and cilantro bunches. Bring to simmering point and simmer for 15 minutes. Add the fish head and water and simmer for 20 minutes. Strain stock and discard solids. Return the stock to a clean saucepan.

**3.** Add the crabs and prawns (shrimp) to the stock, bring to simmer and simmer for 3 minutes. Add the fish and simmer for 1–2 minutes or until all the seafood is cooked.

*Serves 6*

## Lobster Salad with Red Devil Dressing

### INGREDIENTS

1 whole bulb or head garlic

1/3 cup/75mL olive oil

salt

1/2 large onion

2 red bell peppers

1 large portobello mushroom,
   lightly oiled

juice of 1/2 lemon

1 tablespoon/15mL dried fennel

1 tablespoon/15mL tomato sauce
   (ketchup)

1 tablespoon/15mL apple cider vinegar

ground black pepper

1 1/2 lbs/750g cooked lobster tails,
   shredded and chilled

4 cups/1L mixed salad greens

### METHOD

**1.** Preheat the oven to 375°F/190°C. Position the rack in the center of the oven. Lightly oil a baking tray.

**2.** Cut off the top of the garlic and place on a square of aluminum foil. Drizzle with 1 teaspoon/15mL of the olive oil, and sprinkle with a pinch of salt. Wrap in foil, and place on the baking tray. Prepare onion in the same manner.

**3.** Place baking tray in the center of the oven and bake the garlic and onion for 15 minutes. Remove and set aside. Place the red bell peppers on the tray; grill for 15 minutes, turning to blacken all sides. Remove the bell peppers and place in a brown paper bag. Place the mushroom on the baking tray, and grill for 15 minutes. Set the vegetables aside until cool enough to handle.

**4.** Peel and remove the seeds from the bell peppers and place in blender, discarding the seeds and peel. Squeeze the garlic and onion from their skins and add to blender, discarding the skins. Coarsely chop the mushroom and add to the blender along with the remaining olive oil, lemon juice, fennel, tomato sauce (ketchup) and vinegar. Blend until smooth. Season to taste with salt and ground black pepper.

**5.** Place the shredded lobster meat in the center of a large bed of salad greens. Pour the dressing around the lobster meat.

*Serves 3–4*

PRAWN AND CRAB SOUP

# Crab Soup

## INGREDIENTS

**6oz/170g can crabmeat**
**(or fresh, picked crabmeat)**
**1 egg**
**4 dried Chinese mushrooms**
**3oz/85g canned bamboo shoots**
**1 leek**
**small piece fresh ginger**
**1 tablespoon/15mL vegetable oil**
**2 teaspoons/10mL soy sauce**
**1 tablespoon/15mL rice wine, mirin or dry**
**sherry**
**6 cups/1.5L heated stock or water**
**2 teaspoons/10mL salt**
**freshly ground pepper**
**1$^1$/$_2$ tablespoons/25mL cornstarch**
**2 tablespoons/25mL chopped parsley**

## METHOD

**1.** Drain the crabmeat and break up. Beat the egg in a small bowl.

**2.** Soak the dried mushrooms in water for 20 minutes, discard the stalks and slice the caps. Drain the bamboo shoots and cut into strips. Slit the leek almost through, discarding the tough green top, wash carefully, then cut into strips. Grate or finely chop the ginger.

**3.** Heat the oil in a wok or medium-sized saucepan, add the mushrooms, leek, bamboo shoots and ginger and stir-fry for 1 minute.

**4.** Add the crabmeat, sprinkle with soy sauce and rice wine and pour in the heated stock or water. As soon as the liquid comes to the boil, skim off any scum. Season with salt and pepper, stir in the cornstarch mixed with a little water to thicken the soup.

**5.** Pour in the beaten egg and mix, stirring lightly so that the egg sets in short strands. Sprinkle with finely chopped parsley and serve.

*Serves 4–6*

# Crab Salad with Tomato Dressing

## INGREDIENTS

*Dressing*

2 large tomatoes

5 tablespoons/75mL olive oil

1 tablespoon/15mL white wine vinegar

4 tablespoons/60mL light cream

1 teaspoon/5mL chopped fresh tarragon

salt and black pepper

pinch of finely granulated sugar

dash of Worcestershire sauce

2in/5cm piece cucumber, diced

2 large dressed crabs (about 8oz/250g crabmeat)

1 large bulb fennel, thinly sliced, with
feathery top chopped and reserved
to garnish

4 cups/1L mixed salad leaves

1 tablespoon/15mL snipped fresh chives
and paprika or cayenne pepper
to garnish

## METHOD

**1.** To make the dressing, place the tomatoes in a bowl and cover with boiling water. Leave for 30 seconds, then skin, deseed and cut into small dice. Whisk together the oil and vinegar in a bowl, then whisk in the cream, tarragon and seasoning. Add sugar and Worcestershire sauce to taste, then stir in the tomatoes and cucumber.

**2.** Mix together the crabmeat and sliced fennel and stir in 4 tablespoons/60mL of the dressing. Arrange the salad leaves together with the crab mixture on plates. Spoon over the remaining dressing, then sprinkle with the chives, chopped fennel top and paprika or cayenne pepper.

*Serves 4*

# Fresh Crab with a Mustard-Dressed Salad

### INGREDIENTS

*Dressing*

2 tablespoons/25mL Dijon mustard

2 tablespoons/25mL white wine vinegar

6 tablespoons/90mL vegetable oil

pinch of sugar

salt and black pepper

4 small butter lettuces, shredded

3 tablespoons/45mL snipped fresh chives

2 dressed crabs

### METHOD

**1.** To make the dressing, mix together the mustard, vinegar, oil, sugar and seasoning.

**2.** Place the lettuce and 2 tablespoons/25mL of the chives in a bowl, pour over the dressing and toss well. Arrange in bowls, top with the crabmeat and garnish with the remaining chives.

*Serves 4*

Note: Fresh crab is so good that you don't need to do anything too elaborate with it. Buttered brown bread and this simple salad in a light mustard dressing are all you need.

# Hot Crab Salad

### INGREDIENTS

2 tablespoons/25mL oil

1/2 cup/125mL butter

3 cups/750mL mushrooms, sliced

6 shallots, chopped

1/2 red bell pepper, finely diced

1 cup/250mL rice, cooked

4oz/114mL can water chestnuts, cut in half

2 teaspoons/10mL lemon juice

1lb/500g crabmeat

salt and cracked black peppercorns

2 tablespoons/25mL dried parsley flakes

### METHOD

**1.** Heat the oil and butter in a frying pan, sauté the mushrooms, shallots and red bell pepper for 3–5 minutes.

**2.** Add the rice, mix well, and cook, stirring over moderate heat.

**3.** Add the water chestnuts, lemon juice and crabmeat. Season to taste with salt and pepper.

**4.** Sprinkle with parsley to serve.

*Serves 4–6*

FRESH CRAB WITH A
MUSTARD-DRESSED SALAD

## Thai-Style Shellfish and Pomelo Salad

### INGREDIENTS

*Dressing*

1 tablespoon/15mL peanut oil

1 clove garlic, finely chopped

1 shallot, finely chopped

1 red chili, de-seeded and
   finely chopped

2 tablespoons/25mL Thai fish sauce
   (nam pla)

2 tablespoons/25mL soft dark brown
   sugar

juice of 1 lime

1 pomelo or 2 pink grapefruit

1/2 lb/250g cooked peeled prawns
   (shrimp)

170g/6oz can crabmeat in brine,
   drained

1 butter lettuce, chopped

1 green onion, finely chopped

### METHOD

**1.** First make the dressing. Heat the oil in a small frying pan. Fry the garlic, shallot and chili for 3 minutes or until the garlic has turned pale golden and the shallot has softened. Mix together the fish sauce (nam pla), sugar and lime juice, stir in the shallot mixture, then set aside for 5 minutes to cool.

**2.** Using a sharp knife, slice off the top and bottom of the pomelo or grapefruit, then remove the skin and pith, following the curve of the fruit. Cut between the membranes to release the segments.

**3.** Mix the pomelo or grapefruit segments with the prawns (shrimp), crabmeat and lettuce. Pour the dressing over and toss, then sprinkle over the green onion.

*Serves 4*

## Cajun Crab Salad with Honeydew and Cantaloupe

### INGREDIENTS

*Cajun Mayonnaise*

1 medium clove garlic

1 cup/250mL mayonnaise

2 tablespoons/25mL chopped parsley

1 tablespoon/15mL tomato sauce
   (ketchup)

2 teaspoons/10mL drained capers

2 teaspoons/10mL hot spicy mustard

2 teaspoons/10mL horseradish

1/2 teaspoon/2mL dried tarragon

1/2 teaspoon/2mL dried oregano

1/4 teaspoon/1mL Worcestershire sauce

1/8 teaspoon/.5mL cayenne pepper

salt

*Salad*

1lb/500g fresh lump crabmeat

1 medium tomato, seeded and
   cut into 1/4in/5mm dice

1/2 cup/125mL diced celery

4 green onions, cut into 1/4in/5mm pieces

1/4 green bell pepper, cut into
   1/4in/5mm dice

2 tablespoons/25mL lime juice

1 small cantaloupe, peeled,
   seeded and cut into 12 wedges

1 small honeydew melon, peeled,
   seeded and cut into 12 wedges

12 large lettuce leaves

### METHOD

**1.** For the mayonnaise, mince the garlic and blend in all the remaining ingredients.

**2.** Combine all the salad ingredients, except the lettuce, with 1/4 cup/50mL of the mayonnaise. Arrange 2 lettuce leaves on each of 6 plates. Place the crab mixture in the center of the lettuce. Spoon the remaining mayonnaise on the plates and garnish with the melon.

*Serves 4*

# Lobster with Dill

### INGREDIENTS

**2 lobsters weighing about**
**1¹/₂ lbs/750g each**
**few sprigs dill**
**1 lettuce**
**2 slices fresh or unsweetened canned**
**pineapple**
**1¹/₂ cups/375mL button mushrooms**
**1 tablespoon/15mL mayonnaise**
**³/₄ cup/175mL whipping cream, lightly**
**beaten**
**pinch sugar**
**salt and white pepper**

### METHOD

**1.** Prepare the lobsters for cooking and add to a very large pan of boiling, slightly salted water. Cook for 15–20 minutes. Drain, take all the meat out of the shells and claws, and dice. Wash and dry the dill and snip off the small feathery leaves, reserving a sprig or 2 for decoration.

**2.** Wash and dry the lettuce. Drain the pineapple well and cut into small pieces. Slice the mushrooms wafer thin.

**3.** Place all the ingredients except the lettuce and dill in a bowl and mix with the mayonnaise. Fold in the lightly beaten cream, flavored with a pinch of sugar, salt and freshly ground white pepper.

**4.** Line a large salad bowl with the lettuce leaves, spoon in the lobster mixture and decorate with the reserved dill sprigs.

*Serves 4*

# Lobster Pineapple Salad

## INGREDIENTS

**1lb/500g lobster**

**1lb/500g cooked fish fillets**

**1$^{1}/_{2}$ cups/375mL chopped celery**

**$^{2}/_{3}$ cup/150mL chopped almonds**

**14oz/398mL can pineapple chunks**

**$^{3}/_{4}$ cup/175mL mayonnaise**

**1 teaspoon/5mL curry powder**

**$^{1}/_{2}$ teaspoon/2mL salt**

## METHOD

**1.** Dice the lobster, reserving the juice. Break the fish fillets into chunks. Combine the lobster, juice and fish fillets, cover and refrigerate for 10–12 hours.

**2.** Drain the seafood well and add the remaining ingredients. Toss lighty and serve on a bed of lettuce or hollowed-out pineapple halves.

*Serves 6–8*

# Lobster Bisque

## INGREDIENTS

1 small lobster, cooked

1 large carrot, peeled and diced

1 small onion, finely chopped

1/2 cup/125mL butter

3/4 cup/175mL dry white wine

bouquet garni (see Note)

61/2 cups/1.6L fish or chicken stock

3/4 cup/175mL rice

salt, pepper and ground cayenne

1/2 cup/125mL cream

2 tablespoons/25mL brandy

chopped parsley

## METHOD

**1.** Split the lobster in half, lengthwise, and remove the flesh from the shell. Set aside. Wrap the shell in an old tea towel, crush the shell with a hammer and set aside. Sauté the carrot and onion in half the butter until softened without coloring (about 5 minutes). Add the crushed shell, sauté a further minute or so then add the wine. Boil hard until reduced by half. Add the bouquet garni, stock and rice.

**2.** After about 20 minutes, when the rice is tender, remove the large pieces of shell and the bouquet garni. Purée small batches in a food processor with the remainder of the butter, doing so in small batches. Pour through a strainer. Rinse out the food processor to remove every trace of shell and purée the strained liquid again, this time with the lobster flesh, saving a few pieces for the garnish. Reheat gently.

**3.** Taste, add salt, pepper and cayenne to taste then stir in the cream, brandy and reserved lobster pieces, cut into thin slices. Serve very hot garnished with parsley.

*Serves 4*

Note: Bouqet garni is a bunch of herbs, usually sprigs of parsley, thyme, marjoram, rosemary, a bay leaf, peppercorns and cloves, tied in muslin.

## Rock Lobster and Smoked Ocean Trout Salad

**INGREDIENTS**

1 cooked rock lobster

1lb/500g smoked ocean trout

1 English cucumber

1 carrot

1 green zucchini

1 yellow zucchini

1¹/2 cups/375mL tatsoi (bok choy) leaves

1 bunch chives, snipped

*Dressing*

juice of 2 limes

1 tablespoon/15mL brown sugar

¹/2 cup/125mL olive oil

salt and pepper

**METHOD**

**1.** Remove the meat from the tail of the rock lobster, slice finely and set aside. Alternatively ask your fishmonger to do this for you. Cut the smoked ocean trout into thin strips and also set aside.

**2.** Slice the cucumber in half lengthwise and scoop out and discard the seeds. Use a vegetable peeler to make long, skinny strips resembling fettuccine. Peel the carrot and slice in the same manner as the cucumber. Keeping the zucchini whole, also slice them lengthwise into long thin strips.

**3.** Mix the lobster, ocean trout, vegetables and tatsoi leaves gently.

**4.** For the dressing, heat the lime juice and dissolve the brown sugar. Pour into a bowl and whisk in the olive oil until the mixture is thick and the oil has emulsified with the lime juice. Season with salt and pepper and mix this through the salad ingredients.

Arrange the salad on an attractive platter and sprinkle the chives over.

*Serves 4*

Note: Tatsoi is also known as spoon cabbage. It is a leafy Asian green with a slightly spicy cabbage flavor, and is used normally in salads and stir-fries.

## Cream of Crab Soup

**INGREDIENTS**

1 chicken stock (bouillon) cube

1 cup/250mL boiling water

1 small onion, chopped

1 tablespoon/15mL butter

3 tablespoons/45mL flour

¹/4 teaspoon/1mL celery salt

1 teaspoon/5mL black pepper

4 cups/1L milk

1lb/500g crabmeat

chopped parsley

**METHOD**

**1.** Dissolve the stock (bouillon) cube in water. Cook the onion in the butter until tender. Blend in the flour and seasonings. Add the milk and stock gradually and cook until thick, stirring constantly. Add the crabmeat and heat through. Garnish with parsley.

*Serves 4*

# Salad of Lobster
# with Raspberry Dressing

## INGREDIENTS

2 lobster tails, cooked and shells removed

1 small radicchio, leaves separated

1 small butter lettuce, leaves separated

1¹⁄₂cups/375mL snow pea sprouts
  or watercress

1 orange, segmented

12–15 strawberries, halved

### Dressing

4oz/115g fresh or frozen raspberries

2 tablespoons/25mL raspberry vinegar

2 tablespoons/25mL vegetable oil

1 teaspoon/5mL finely chopped fresh mint

1 tablespoon/15mL sugar

## METHOD

**1.** Cut the lobster tails into ¹⁄₂in/1cm medallions
and set aside.

**2.** Arrange the radicchio, lettuce, sprouts or
watercress, lobster, orange segments and
strawberries attractively on a serving platter
and refrigerate until required.

**3.** To make the dressing, place the raspberries in
a food processor or blender and process until
pureed. Push through a sieve to remove the
seeds. Combine the raspberry puree with the
vinegar, oil, mint and sugar. Mix well to combine,
pour over the salad and serve immediately.

*Serves 4*

Note: Lobster would have to be the
undisputed king of shellfish. In this
recipe, it is taken to new heights with
the addition of a raspberry dressing.

# Creamy Lobster Chowder

## INGREDIENTS

1/4 cup/50mL quick cooking rice

1 teaspoon/5mL salt

1/4 teaspoon/1mL pepper

1/4 teaspoon/1mL paprika

1 tablespoon/15mL onion, finely minced

1 small red bell pepper, diced

2 stalks celery, chopped

2 cups/500mL milk

2 cups/500mL light cream

3/4 lb/375g lobster meat, diced

2 tablespoons/25mL butter

2 tablespoons/25mL parsley, chopped

## METHOD

**1.** Combine the rice, salt, pepper, paprika, onion, bell pepper, celery, milk and cream in a saucepan. Cook over medium heat, stirring frequently, for 10–12 minutes, or until the rice softens.

**2.** Stir in the lobster and butter. Remove from the heat, cool and store in the refrigerator. Just before serving, stir through the parsley then reheat the chowder over medium heat, stirring frequently.

*Serves 4–6*

Note: This chowder is best aged for at least five hours before serving, so prepare the dish well ahead of time.

# Tarragon Seafood Salad

## INGREDIENTS

4 tablespoons/60mL chopped fresh
   tarragon

2 tablespoons/25mL lime juice

3 teaspoons/15mL grated lime rind

1 fresh red chili, chopped

2 teaspoons/10mL olive oil

freshly ground black pepper, to taste

1lb/500g uncooked lobster tail, flesh
   removed from shell and cut into large
   pieces or 1lb/500g firm white fish
   fillets, cut into large pieces

3 cups/750mL snow pea sprouts or
   watercress

1 cucumber, sliced into ribbons

2 carrots, sliced into ribbons

1 red bell pepper, cut into thin strips

## METHOD

**1.** Place the tarragon, lime juice, lime rind, chili, oil and black pepper in a bowl and mix to combine. Add lobster or fish fillets, toss to coat and set aside to marinate for 15 minutes.

**2.** Arrange the snow pea sprouts or watercress, cucumber, carrot and red bell pepper on a large serving platter and set aside.

**3.** Heat a char-grill or frying pan over a high heat, add the lobster mixture and cook, turning frequently, for 2 minutes or until the lobster is tender. Arrange the lobster over salad, spoon over the pan juices and serve immediately.

*Serves 4*

Note: To make cucumber and carrot ribbons, use a vegetable peeler to remove strips lengthwise from the cucumber or carrot. This salad is also delicious made using prawns instead of lobster. If using prawns, shell and devein them before marinating.

# Spiced Crab Soup

## INGREDIENTS

2 cups/500mL water

2 tablespoons/25mL Denjang paste
   (fermented soyabean)

1 cup/250mL soft bean curd or tofu, in
   $^{1}/_{2}$in/1cm cube

1 teaspoon/5mL hot red chili powder,
   mixed with 1 tablespoon/15mL water

1 slice fresh ginger

1 small onion, sliced

1 garlic clove, crushed

2 crabs, each in 4 pieces

1 zucchini, sliced

## METHOD

**1.** Put the water and Denjang paste into a pan and simmer over low heat, covered, for 10 minutes. Add the bean curd and cook for 5 minutes more.

**2.** Now add all the other ingredients and cook for 15 minutes more. Serve in four individual bowls with rice and an assortment of side dishes.

*Serves 4*

TARRAGON SEAFOOD SALAD

## Lobster Rice Salad

### INGREDIENTS

6oz/170g lobster meat, diced

$2^{1}/_{2}$ cups/625mL cooked rice

1 tablespoon/15mL lemon juice

$1^{1}/_{2}$ cups/375mL celery, finely diced

$^{1}/_{4}$ cup/50mL green bell pepper, finely
diced

$^{1}/_{2}$ cup/125mL crushed pineapple, drained

1 teaspoon/5mL salt

$^{1}/_{2}$ teaspoon/2mL black pepper

$^{1}/_{2}$ cup/125mL mayonnaise

### METHOD

**1.** Combine all the ingredients. Place in a
bowl or mold. Chill for several hours.
Turn out onto a bed of lettuce.

*Serves 6*

## Crab, Mango and Cucumber Salad

### INGREDIENTS

1lb/500g fresh lump crabmeat, picked
over for shells and cartilage

$1^{1}/_{2}$ tablespoons/20mL freshly squeezed
lime juice

3 tablespoons/45mL extra-virgin olive oil

1 tablespoon/15mL finely chopped
cilantro, plus 4 whole leaves
for garnish

2 teaspoons/10mL finely chopped mint
leaves, plus 4 whole leaves for garnish

salt and freshly ground white pepper

hot chili sauce

1 medium mango, peeled, pitted,
and cut into $^{1}/_{4}$in/5mm dice

1 cucumber, peeled, seeded and
cut into $^{1}/_{4}$in/5mm dice

1 tablespoon/15mL unsalted peanuts,
toasted and roughly chopped

### METHOD

**1.** Season the crabmeat with $^{1}/_{2}$ of the lime
juice, $^{1}/_{2}$ of the olive oil, $^{2}/_{3}$ of the chopped
cilantro and mint, salt and pepper to taste
and about 10 drops of hot chili sauce. Toss
the crabmeat lightly with a fork or your
fingers. If you wish to serve the salad
family-style, put the crab in a chilled shallow
bowl. For individual servings, arrange the
crab in 4 chilled shallow soup plates.

**2.** Season the mango and cucumber with the
remaining lime juice, olive oil, chopped
cilantro and mint, salt and pepper to taste
and about 10 drops of hot chili sauce. Mix
well and scatter the mixture over the
crabmeat, in either large or small bowls.
Sprinkle the salad with the chopped peanuts
and top with the whole cilantro and mint
leaves. Serve mango coulis on the side, if
desired.

*Serves 4*

LOBSTER RICE SALAD

# Lobster and Sprout Salad

## INGREDIENTS

1¹/₂ cups/375mL mayonnaise

¹/₂ cup/125mL Pernod

4 large sorrel leaves, finely shredded

¹/₄ cup/50mL finely chopped celery

¹/₄ teaspoon/1mL chili sauce

1lb/500g cooked lobster

snow pea sprouts or watercress

## METHOD

**1.** Combine the mayonnaise, Pernod, sorrel, celery and chili sauce. Chop the lobster into bite-sized pieces and arrange them on the sprouts or watercress. Spoon over the sauce. Serve with thin slices of buttered wholegrain bread.

*Serves 4 6*

# APPETIZERS & SNACKS

# Lobster Filo Triangles

## INGREDIENTS

### Lobster Cream Filling

1 cooked lobster

3 tablespoons/45mL butter

6 green onions, chopped

2 cloves garlic, crushed

1$^{1}/_{2}$ tablespoons/25mL flour

$^{1}/_{4}$ cup/50mL white wine

$^{1}/_{4}$ cup/50mL heavy or whipping cream

pinch of cayenne pepper

freshly ground black pepper


8 sheets filo pastry

$^{1}/_{2}$ cup/125mL butter, melted and cooled

## METHOD

**1.** To make the filling, remove the meat from the lobster, chop finely and set aside. Melt butter in a saucepan over a medium heat, add green onions and garlic and cook, stirring, until the onions are tender. Stir in the flour and cook for 1 minute.

**2.** Remove the pan from the heat and whisk in the wine and the cream, a little at a time, until well blended. Season to taste with cayenne and black pepper, return to the heat and cook, stirring constantly, until the sauce boils and thickens. Reduce the heat to low and simmer for 3 minutes. Remove from the heat, stir in the lobster meat and cool completely.

**3.** Cut the pastry sheets lengthwise into 2in/5cm wide strips. Working with one strip of pastry at a time, brush the pastry with melted butter. Place a teaspoonful of the filling on one end of the strip, fold the corner of the pastry diagonally over the filling, then continue folding up the strip to make a neat triangle.

**4.** Place the triangles on a baking tray, brush with butter and bake in a moderate oven at 350°F/180°C for 10–15 minutes or until golden.

*Makes 24*

# Scampi Sashimi

## INGREDIENTS

**8 scampi (if unavailable fresh, frozen is also good)**

*Chirizu (Spicy Dipping Sauce)*
**5 teaspoons/25mL sake**
**3 tablespoons/45mL freshly grated daikon radish**
**2 green onions, finely sliced**
**3 tablespoons/45mL soy sauce**
**3 tablespoons/45mL lemon juice**
**$1/8$ teaspoon/.5mL hichimi togarashi (seven-pepper spice)**

## METHOD

**1.** To prepare the scampi, remove the heads and set aside for garnish. Peel back the underside shell from the top down to the tail. Remove the flesh and discard the shells except for the bottom part of tail. Place the scampi meat on a plate, putting the head and tail on as a garnish.

**2.** To make the dipping sauce, warm the sake in a small saucepan, remove it from the heat and quickly ignite it with a match, and shake the pan gently until the flame dies out. Allow to cool.

**3.** Combine the sake with the other ingredients and mix well. Pour into individual bowls and serve with the scampi (or any other sashimi).

*Serves 6*

Note: The scampi, or deep sea lobster as it is also called, has a wonderfully sweet flesh, ideal for sashimi. It is considered by many to have eating qualities above that of the lobster.

# Lobster Topping

## INGREDIENTS

**4oz/125g cream cheese**

**$1/2$ cup/125mL mayonnaise**

**$1/4$ cup/50mL sour cream**

**2 tablespoons/25mL lobster juice**

**2 teaspoons/10mL lemon juice**

**$1/2$ clove garlic, crushed**

**1 teaspoon/5mL dried chives**

**$1/2$ lb/250g lobster meat, diced**

## METHOD

Beat together the cream cheese, mayonnaise and sour cream. Add the lobster juice, lemon juice, garlic and chives. Beat well. Stir in the lobster. Serve over hot baked potatoes.

*Serves 6–8*

## Crabmeat Soufflé

### INGREDIENTS

3 tablespoons/45mL butter

3 tablespoons/45mL flour

1 cup/250mL milk

salt and freshly ground pepper

pinch of cayenne

7 1/2 oz/213mL can crabmeat, drained and
  flaked

1/4 cup/50mL flaked almonds

4 egg yolks

5 egg whites

### METHOD

**1.** Prepare a 6 cup/1.5mL soufflé mold or
four individual dishes. Set the oven at
375°F/190°C. Heat a metal tray in the oven.

**2.** Melt the butter in a saucepan and stir in
the flour. Cook over low heat for 1 minute.
Gradually add the milk and cook, stirring, until
thickened. Season to taste with salt, pepper
and cayenne and fold in the crabmeat and
almonds. Add the egg yolks, one at a time.
Whip the egg whites until stiff, then fold into
the mixture. Pour into the prepared soufflé dish
or dishes, place on a metal tray and bake for
about 25 minutes (18 minutes for individual
ones) or until puffed and golden.

*Serves 4*

## Devilled Lobster

### INGREDIENTS

1 1/4 lbs/625g lobster, steamed,
  tail, leg and claw meat separated

1/4 teaspoon/1mL garlic, minced

1/2 tablespoon/7mL horseradish, fresh

1/2 tablespoon/7mL prepared brown
  mustard

1/2 tablespoon/7mL lemon juice

1 teaspoon/5mL dill weed

1/4 teaspoon/1mL sweet chili sauce

3/4 cup/175mL mayonnaise

fresh ground pepper, to taste

18 large eggs, hard-boiled, sliced in
  half and yolks removed

slivered black olives, to garnish

### METHOD

**1.** Cut the lobster meat into small 1/2in/1cm
chunks. Then place all the ingredients
including the egg yolks (with the exception of
the white egg halves and olives), in a food
processor or blender and blend until slightly
smooth.

**2.** Fill a piping bag with the blended
ingredients and squeeze into the egg halves,
sprinkle with ground pepper and garnish with
the slivered black olives. Refrigerate until
ready to use.

*Makes 36*

CRABMEAT SOUFFLÉ

# Crab-Stuffed Mushrooms

## INGREDIENTS

**8 mushrooms (each about 2in/5cm**
**diameter), stems removed**
**French dressing, for marinating**
**1/2lb/250g crabmeat**
**2 tablespoons/25mL finely chopped red**
**bell pepper**
**2 tablespoons/25mL finely chopped celery**
**1 teaspoon/5mL lemon juice**
**1/4 teaspoon/1mL Dijon mustard**
**chopped fresh dill**
**2 tablespoons/25mL sour cream**
**3 tablespoons/45mL mayonnaise**

## METHOD

**1.** Marinate the mushrooms in the French
dressing for about 30 minutes.

**2.** Place the crabmeat, bell pepper and celery in a
bowl. Lightly mix together.

**3.** Blend the remaining ingredients together,
and mix through the crab mixture. Chill.

**4.** Just before serving, drain the mushroom caps
and fill with the crab mixture.

*Serves 4*

## Crabmeat Ramekins

### INGREDIENTS

1lb/500g crabmeat

3 strips bacon

1 teaspoon/5mL mustard powder

1 teaspoon/5mL ground paprika

1 teaspoon/5mL celery salt

2 drops Tabasco sauce

2 tablespoons/25mL sweet chili sauce

1 teaspoon/5mL white wine vinegar

1 cup/250mL mayonnaise

parsley, for garnish

### METHOD

**1.** Preheat the oven to 350°F/180°C.

**2.** Divide the crab among 6 greased ramekins and place in the oven to heat through.

**3.** Chop the bacon, fry until crisp, then sprinkle over the crab.

**4.** Combine the mustard, paprika, celery salt, Tabasco sauce, chili sauce, vinegar and mayonnaise.

**5.** Spoon over the crabmeat, and brown under a hot griller until golden. Garnish with chopped parsley.

*Serves 4*

# Lobster Croquettes

## INGREDIENTS

**1lb/500g lobster meat**
**1/2 teaspoon/2mL pepper**
**1/2 teaspoon/2mL salt**
**pinch of mace**
**1 cup/250mL breadcrumbs**
**1/2 cup/50mL butter, melted**
**1 egg, beaten**
**6 crackers, crushed**
**lard, for cooking**
**chopped parsley, for garnish**

## METHOD

**1.** Chop the lobster meat, add pepper, salt and a pinch of mace.

**2.** Mix with this about a quarter as much breadcrumbs as you have meat. Add enough melted butter to shape them into pointed balls.

**3.** Roll in the beaten egg, then in the crushed crackers, and fry in boiling lard.

**4.** Serve very hot, garnished with the parsley.

*Serves 4*

Note: This is a delicious dish for a luncheon or entrée.

## Lobster Toasts

### INGREDIENTS

8oz/250g cream cheese
1/4 cup/50mL unsalted butter
2oz/50g cooked lobster meat
1 tablespoon/15mL olive oil
juice of 1/2 lemon
salt and pepper, to taste
12 slices of French baguette,
   or Turkish bread, toasted
fresh parsley, chopped, for garnish
extra olive oil, for serving

### METHOD

**1.** Combine all the ingredients, except toast and parsley in a food processor and blend until creamy.

**2.** Spread on the toast and heat through under a preheated hot grill before serving.

**3.** Sprinkle with chopped parsley and ground black pepper, drizzle with some olive oil and serve.

*Serves 6*

# Crabmeat Fritters

## INGREDIENTS

3 eggs

1 cup/250mL bean sprouts

3 green onions, chopped

3/4lb/375g crabmeat

salt and cracked black peppercorns

oil, for deep frying

*Sauce*

2 teaspoons/10mL cornstarch

1 tablespoon/15mL sugar

3 tablespoons/45mL soy sauce

1 cup/250mL chicken stock

2 tablespoons/25mL dry sherry

## METHOD

**1.** Beat the eggs in a bowl, stir in the bean sprouts, green onions and crabmeat, and add salt and pepper to taste.

**2.** Heat sufficient oil to cover the base of a frying pan, and drop in all of the crab mixture, a heaped tablespoon at a time.

**3.** Fry until golden brown on one side, then turn and brown the other side.

**4.** Remove from the pan and keep warm.

**5.** For the sauce, blend together the cornstarch and sugar in a pan then add the soy sauce and chicken stock.

**6.** Slowly bring to the boil over a low heat, stirring all the time. Cook for 3 minutes, or until sauce is thickened. Stir in the sherry.

*Serves 4*

# Lobster Cocktail

## INGREDIENTS

1/2 cup/50mL horseradish

11/2 cups/375mL bottled tomato sauce

2 tablespoons/25mL fresh lemon juice

2 tablespoons/25mL Worcestershire
   sauce

1 small head iceberg lettuce, outer
   leaves removed

1lb/500g lobster meat,
   cut into bite-sized pieces

1 lemon, quartered lengthwise

## METHOD

**1.** Make the cocktail sauce by combining the first 4 ingredients in a small bowl. Stir until thoroughly blended, cover with plastic wrap and refrigerate until ready to use.

**2.** With a sharp knife make clean vertical cuts in the lettuce from top to bottom, thinly slicing the head of the lettuce into loose strips or chiffonnade.

**3.** Cover each salad plate or glass soup plate with the sliced lettuce. Spoon 1/4 cup/50mL of cocktail sauce into the center of each lettuce nest. Arrange a quarter of the chilled lobster pieces in a circle around the sauce on each plate. Garnish each dish with a lemon wedge and cocktail fork. Serve immediately.

*Serves 4*

# CRABMEAT FRITTERS

# Scampi with Basil Butter

## INGREDIENTS

**8 uncooked scampi, heads removed**

*Basil Butter*
**1/3 cup/75mL butter, melted**
**2 tablespoons/25mL chopped fresh
basil**
**1 clove garlic, crushed**
**2 teaspoons/10mL honey**

## METHOD

**1.** Cut the scampi in half, lengthwise.

**2.** To make the basil butter, place the butter, basil, garlic and honey in a small bowl and whisk to combine.

**3.** Brush the cut side of each scampi half with basil butter and cook under a preheated hot grill for 2 minutes or until they change color and are tender.

**4.** Drizzle with any remaining basil butter and serve immediately.

*Serves 4*

# Sea Captain's Dip

## INGREDIENTS

**4oz/125g cream cheese**

**2 tablespoons/25mL lemon juice**

**1/4 cup/50mL mayonnaise**

**1/4 teaspoon/1mL garlic salt**

**2 tablespoons/25mL onion, diced**

**1 teaspoon/5mL dried chives**

**6oz/170g lobster meat, finely diced**

## METHOD

**1.** Cream the cream cheese and lemon juice. Add the mayonnaise, garlic salt, onion, chives and lobster and mix well.

**2.** Chill at least for 6 hours, then serve with crackers or fresh vegetables.

*Makes 2 cups/500mL*

# Lobster Crêpes

## INGREDIENTS

### Filling

1lb/500g lobster meat, fresh or frozen

1/4 cup/50g butter

2 tablespoons/25mL onion, chopped

1lb/500g mushrooms, sliced

1/2 cup/125mL all-purpose flour

1/2 teaspoon/2mL salt

pinch of pepper

1 cup/250mL milk

### Crêpes

2 eggs

1 1/2 cups/375mL all-purpose flour

1/2 teaspoon/2mL salt

1 teaspoon/5mL dried parsley

1 teaspoon/5mL dried chives

1 cup/250mL milk

1/4 cup/50g butter, melted

1/4 cup/50g Swiss cheese, grated

## METHOD

**1.** If frozen, thaw, and chop the lobster into bite-sized pieces. Melt the butter and sauté the onion and the mushrooms for 3–5 minutes. Stir in the flour and seasonings, add the milk and cook, stirring constantly until thickened. Add the lobster.

**2.** To make the crêpes, beat the eggs, add the flour and seasonings. Add the milk and beat until smooth. Refrigerate for 2 hours. For each crêpe, pour 2–3 tablespoons/ 25–45mL of batter into a heated, oiled pan. Brown lightly on each side.

**3.** Spoon 3 tablespoons/45mL of filling into each crêpe, roll up and arrange in a baking dish. Brush with half the melted butter and sprinkle with the grated cheese. Bake at 425°F/220°C for 5–8 minutes. Stir the remaining melted butter into the remaining filling and serve over the crêpes.

*Serves 6*

# Lobster Puffs

## INGREDIENTS

1lb/500g lobster meat

4oz/125g cream cheese

1 tablespoon/15mL mayonnaise

1/2 tablespoon/7mL Worcestershire sauce

1/2 teaspoon/2mL salt

1 dash pepper, to taste

1 loaf Italian bread, sliced 1/2 in/1cm thick

## METHOD

**1.** Mix all of the ingredients, except the bread, in a mixing bowl. Remove the crust from each bread slice and then toast. Cut the bread into 2in/5cm triangles, squares and/or round shapes using a biscuit cutter or knife. Lay the bread onto a baking tray or griller pan.

**2.** Spread the lobster mixture over the bread shapes approximately 1/4in/5mm thick. Place under a griller for 1 minute to brown just before serving. Transfer to a serving dish and enjoy.

*Serves 4*

LOBSTER CRÊPES

## Grilled Scampi with Herb Butter

### INGREDIENTS

10–12 scampi

$2/3$ cup/150mL butter

few sprigs fresh herbs, chopped

2 tablespoons/25mL chopped parsley

2 cloves garlic, finely chopped

salt and freshly ground pepper

lemon wedges

### METHOD

**1.** Split the scampi lengthwise through the center and arrange, cut side up, on a large shallow dish. Melt the butter and add the herbs and garlic. Drizzle the flavored butter over the scampi and season with freshly ground pepper. (The scampi can be prepared ahead up to this stage.)

**2.** Preheat the griller and arrange the scampi, cut side up, on the grilling pan. Cook for about 5 minutes until the flesh has turned white. Remove from the heat, season with salt and arrange on a large serving platter with wedges of lemon. To eat the scampi use a fork to pull out the tail meat.

**3.** Place a bowl on the table for the discarded shells, and a few finger bowls, each with a squeeze of lemon.

*Serves 4*

# Rice Cakes with Lime Crab

## INGREDIENTS

1³/4 cups/425mL jasmine rice, cooked
1 cup/250mL fresh cilantro, chopped
crushed black peppercorns
vegetable oil, for deep-frying

*Lime Crab Topping*

7¹/2 oz/213mL canned crabmeat, well drained
2 fresh red chilies, seeded and chopped
2 small fresh green chilies, finely sliced
¹/4 cup/50mL coconut cream
2 tablespoons/25mL thick plain yogurt
3 teaspoons/15mL lime juice
3 teaspoons/15mL Thai fish sauce (nam pla)
3 teaspoons/15mL finely grated lime rind
1 tablespoon/15mL crushed black peppercorns

## METHOD

**1.** Combine the rice, cilantro and black peppercorns to taste, then press into an oiled 7in x 11in/18cm x 28cm shallow cake tin and refrigerate until set. Cut the rice mixture into 1¹/4in x 1¹/2in/3cm x 4cm rectangles.

**2.** Heat the vegetable oil in a large saucepan until a cube of bread dropped in browns in 50 seconds and cook the rice cakes, a few at a time, for 3 minutes or until golden. Drain on absorbent paper towels.

**3.** To make the topping, place the crabmeat, red and green chilies, coconut cream, yogurt, lime juice and fish sauce in a food processor and process until smooth. Stir in the lime rind and black peppercorns. Serve with warm rice cakes.

*Makes 24*

## Lobster Sashimi

### INGREDIENTS

**1 whole green (uncooked) lobster**

**shredded daikon radish**

**endive, for garnish**

**shredded carrot, for garnish**

### METHOD

**1.** If the lobster is purchased frozen, allow it to defrost overnight in the refrigerator.

**2.** Remove the head and reserve for garnish.

**3.** Use poultry scissors to make a nice clean cut in the tail shell.

**4.** Pull the lobster meat out. Stuff the empty shell with the shredded daikon radish for presentation. Cut the lobster into small sashimi slices.

**5.** Lay the meat on the daikon-bedded tail. Garnish with the endive and shredded carrot and serve.

*Serves 4*

Note: Traditionally, lobsters that were to be prepared as sashimi were purchased live and killed moments before being presented and served. The Japanese obsession with absolute freshness has made this practice commonplace.

# Lobster-Stuffed Potatoes

## INGREDIENTS

**6 potatoes, baked**

**1 tablespoon/15mL butter, softened**

**$1/2$ cup/125mL sour cream**

**$1/4$ cup/50mL onion, grated**

**$1/4$ teaspoon/1mL pepper**

**$1/4$ lb/125g lobster meat, diced**

**$3/4$ cup/175mL mushrooms, diced**

**1 cup/250mL Cheddar cheese, grated**

## METHOD

**1.** Preheat the oven to 375°F/190°C.

**2.** Cut the baked potatoes in half lengthwise and carefully scoop out the insides, reserving the skins.

**3.** In a bowl, mash the potato, then add the butter, sour cream, onion and pepper. Beat until smooth. Fold in the lobster meat and mushrooms and place the mixture back in the 12 potato skin halves. Sprinkle with the grated cheese and place on a baking tray.

**4.** Bake for 15–20 minutes, or until the potatoes are heated through.

*Serves 6*

## Lobster Cheese Rolls

### INGREDIENTS

2/3 cup/150mL celery, chopped

2 tablespoons/25mL onion, minced

1/2 cup/125mL mayonnaise

1 tablespoon/15mL French dressing

1 cup/250mL Cheddar cheese, grated

1/2 cup/125mL slivered almonds, toasted

2 teaspoons/10mL lemon juice

1/2 teaspoon/2mL salt

6 buttered rolls

1lb/500g cooked lobster meat, sliced

### METHOD

**1.** Combine the first 8 ingredients and toss lightly to combine. Top one half of each roll with the lobster and some celery mixture then cover with the other roll half. Wrap in aluminium foil and place in a preheated 350°F/180°C oven for 8–10 minutes.

*Serves 6*

## Crab Puffs

### INGREDIENTS

2 tablespoons/25mL butter

2 tablespoons/25mL flour

1/2 teaspoon/2mL salt

dash of pepper

1 cup/250mL milk

2 egg yolks, beaten

1/4 teaspoon/1mL paprika

1lb/500g crabmeat

1 cup whipping cream

2 egg whites, beaten

### METHOD

**1.** Melt the butter then blend in the flour and seasonings. Add the milk gradually and cook until thick, stirring constantly. Stir a little of the hot sauce into the egg yolks. Add to the remaining sauce, stirring constantly. Add the paprika and crabmeat. Whip cream then fold in along with egg whites.

**2.** Place in 6 well greased individual 10fl oz/285mL casserole dishes in a baking dish of hot water. Bake in a preheated moderate 350°F/180°C oven for 40 minutes.

*Serves 4*

LOBSTER CHEESE ROLLS

# Lobster Crowns

## INGREDIENTS

24 large mushrooms
1/4 teaspoon/1mL salt
dash pepper
2 tablespoons/25mL butter
1 tablespoon/15mL onion, finely diced
2 tablespoons/25mL mushroom stems,
  finely diced

1 teaspoon/5mL butter, extra
1/4 lb/125g lobster meat, diced
1 cup/250mL Cheddar cheese, grated

## METHOD

1. Remove the stems from the mushrooms. Sprinkle the caps with salt and pepper and fry for 5 minutes in butter over medium heat. Combine the onion, mushroom stems, extra butter and lobster. Stuff the caps with the mixture, and sprinkle with grated cheese.

2. Grill for 4–5 minutes.

*Serves 4*

# MAIN MEALS

# Garlic Lobster Tails with Exotic Salad

## INGREDIENTS

*Honey and Lemon Marinade*

1/2 cup/125mL olive oil

2 tablespoons/25mL lemon juice

1 tablespoon/15mL honey

1 tablespoon/15mL freshly crushed garlic

2 bay leaves, crushed


6 green (raw) lobster tails

1/3 cup/75mL butter, softened

2 teaspoons/10mL crushed garlic

2 tablespoons/25mL Honey and
   Lemon Marinade


*Exotic Salad*

1 avocado, cut into 1/4in/5mm dice

2 Lebanese cucumbers (or 1 English
   cucumber), diced

1/2 small cantaloupe, peeled and diced

1/3 cup/75mL Honey and Lemon Marinade

## METHOD

**1.** Prepare the marinade by combining all ingredients well. Set aside.

**2.** With kitchen scissors, cut each side of the soft shell on the underside of the lobster tails, and remove. Run a metal skewer through the length of each tail to keep them flat while cooking. Soften the butter and mix in the garlic and the Honey and Lemon Marinade. Spread a coating on the lobster meat.

**3.** Prepare the salad before starting to cook the lobster tails. Mix the diced avocado, cucumber and cantaloupe together. Pour the marinade over the salad. Refrigerate until needed.

**4.** Heat the barbecue to medium-high and oil the grill bars. Place the lobster tails shell-side down and cook until the shell turns red. Spread with more butter and turn meat-side down and cook for 5–8 minutes or until the meat turns white. Turn again and cook for 2 minutes more, shell-side down. Remove the skewers and place the lobster on warm plates. Dot with any remaining butter mixture and serve immediately with the Exotic Salad.

*Serves 4–6*

# Grilled Lobster with Chili Salsa

## INGREDIENTS

### Salsa

2 tablespoons/125mL olive oil

1 red bell pepper,
   de-seeded and diced

1 small onion, chopped

1 large red chili, de-seeded
   and finely chopped

1 tablespoon/15mL sun-dried tomato paste

salt and black pepper

2 cooked lobsters (about
   $^1/_2$lb/375mL each)

4 teaspoons/20mL olive oil

cayenne pepper

## METHOD

**1.** To make the salsa, heat the oil in a saucepan and fry the red bell pepper, onion and chili for 5 minutes or until tender. Stir in the tomato paste and season to taste. Transfer to a bowl.

**2.** To cut the lobsters in half lengthwise, turn on their backs. Cut through the head end first, using a large, sharp knife, then turn the lobsters around and cut through the tail end. Discard the small greyish sac in the head – everything else in the shell is edible. Crack the large claws with a small hammer or wooden rolling pin. Drizzle the cut side of the lobsters with the oil and sprinkle with the cayenne pepper.

**3.** Heat a large non-stick frying pan or ridged cast iron grill pan until very hot, then add the lobster halves, cut-side down, and cook for 2–3 minutes, until lightly golden. Serve with the salsa.

*Serves 2*

## Lobster Abegweit

### INGREDIENTS

**3 tablespoons/45mL butter**

**1lb/500g lobster meat, diced**

**3 cups/750mL mushrooms, sliced**

**1 tablespoon/15mL onion, diced**

**3 tablespoons/45mL flour**

**1 teaspoon/5mL salt**

**13oz/385mL can evaporated milk**

**1/2 cup/125mL whole milk**

**1/4 cup/50mL processed cheese spread**

**2 tablespoons/25mL parsley, chopped**

**pasta of choice, cooked**

### METHOD

**1.** Melt the butter, add the lobster meat and sauté for 5 minutes. Add the mushrooms and onion, and sauté an additional 5 minutes. Stir in the flour, salt, evaporated milk and whole milk. Cook, stirring constantly until thick and smooth. Stir in the cheese spread and parsley.

**2.** Toss through hot cooked pasta and serve.

*Serves 6*

## Cognac Lobster with Basil Butter

### INGREDIENTS

***Basil Butter***

**1/2 cup/125mL butter, roughly chopped**

**2 tablespoons/25mL finely chopped fresh basil leaves**

**2 teaspoons/10mL finely chopped fresh parsley**

**freshly ground black pepper**

**3 tablespoons/45mL cognac**

**2lbs/1kg uncooked lobsters, halved and cleaned**

**2 tablespoons/25mL lemon juice**

**2 tablespoons/25mL olive oil**

**freshly ground black pepper**

### METHOD

**1.** To make the basil butter, beat the butter until smooth. Stir in the basil and parsley and season to taste with black pepper. Place in a small bowl and refrigerate until required.

**2.** Drizzle the lobsters with lemon juice and brush the flesh with oil. Cook under a hot grill or on a barbecue, shell-side first, for 5 minutes. Turn over and cook for 5–10 minutes, or until the flesh is just cooked. Brush with extra oil, if necessary, during cooking.

**3.** Remove the lobsters from the heat. Remove the flesh from the tails in one piece and cut into pieces. Pile back into the shells and set aside to keep warm. Warm the cognac by holding a lighted match over it. As soon as it ignites, spoon over the lobster.

**4.** Divide the basil butter into 4 portions and place one piece on each lobster half.

*Serves 4*

LOBSTER ABEGWEIT

# Crab in Creamy Tomato Sauce

## INGREDIENTS

2 tablespoons/25mL butter

12 cherry tomatoes

6 green onions, chopped

3 teaspoons/15mL freshly crushed garlic

2lb/1kg crabmeat

1/2 cup/125mL fresh parsley, chopped

2 tablespoons/25mL lemon juice

2 tablespoons/25mL tomato paste

1 cup/250g light cream

salt and pepper

pasta of choice, cooked

## METHOD

**1.** Melt the butter in a frying pan. Add the cherry tomatoes, green onions and garlic and sauté for 3 minutes. Reduce the heat to low, stir in the crabmeat, and parsley, and cook over low heat for 2 minutes.

**2.** Stir in the lemon juice, tomato paste and cream. Season with salt and pepper. Heat gently.

**3.** Serve over hot cooked pasta.

*Serves 4–6*

# Crab Casserole

## INGREDIENTS

1¹/₂ tablespoons/20g butter

1 onion, chopped

1 green bell pepper, diced

14oz/400g crabmeat

1 cup/250mL mayonnaise

4 hard-boiled eggs, chopped

1 cup/250mL cooked rice

1¹/₂ cups/375mL fresh bread, cut into cubes

1 tablespoon/15mL parsley flakes

¹/₄ cup/50mL butter, melted

## METHOD

**1.** Preheat the oven to 350°F/180°C.

**2.** Heat the butter in a pan, add the onion and bell pepper, and stir over a moderate heat, until the onions are soft.

**3.** Stir in the crab, mayonnaise, eggs and rice.

**4.** Spoon the mixture into an ovenproof dish. Mix together the bread cubes, parsley and melted butter.

**5.** Sprinkle the breadcrumb mix over the crab mixture. Bake for 20–25 minutes.

*Serves 4*

# Bouillabaisse

## INGREDIENTS

6¹/₂ lb/3kg mixed seafood, including firm
   white fish fillets, prawns (shrimp),
   mussels, crab and calamari (squid) rings
¹/₄ cup/50mL olive oil
2 cloves garlic, crushed
2 large onions, chopped
2 leeks, sliced
2 x 14oz/398mL canned tomatoes,
   undrained and mashed
1 tablespoon/15mL chopped fresh thyme
   or 1 teaspoon/5mL dried thyme
2 tablespoons/25mL chopped fresh basil
   or 1¹/₂ teaspoons/7mL dried basil
2 tablespoons/25mL chopped fresh parsley
2 bay leaves
2 tablespoons/25mL finely grated orange
   rind
1 teaspoon/5mL saffron threads
1 cup/250mL dry white wine
1 cup/250mL fish stock
freshly ground black pepper

## METHOD

**1.** Remove the bones and skin from the fish fillets and cut into ³/₄in/2cm cubes. Peel and devein the prawns (shrimp), leaving the tails intact. Scrub and remove the beards from the mussels. Cut the crab into quarters. Set aside.

**2.** Heat the oil in a large saucepan over a medium heat, add the garlic, onions and leeks and cook for 5 minutes or until the onions are golden. Add the tomatoes, thyme, basil, parsley, bay leaves, orange rind, saffron, wine and stock and bring to the boil. Reduce the heat and simmer for 30 minutes.

**3.** Add the fish and crab and cook for 10 minutes. Add the remaining seafood and cook for 5 minutes longer or until everything is cooked. Season to taste with black pepper.

*Serves 6*

# Crab with Ginger

## INGREDIENTS

2 x 26oz/750g or 1 x 3$^1/_3$lb/1.5kg
   fresh crab
1 tablespoon/15mL corn oil
2in/5cm fresh peeled ginger, thinly
   sliced and cut into strips
1 teaspoon/5mL crushed garlic
5 shallots, cut into 2in/5cm pieces
1 cup/250mL fish stock
1 tablespoon/15mL dry sherry
1 teaspoon/5mL oyster sauce
$^1/_2$ teaspoon/2mL Worcestershire sauce
1 tablespoon/15mL soy sauce
$^1/_2$ teaspoon/2mL sugar
2 teaspoons/10mL cornstarch, mixed with
   1 tablespoon/15mL cold water
1 teaspoon/5mL sesame oil
1 red chili, slivered, for garnish
boiled rice, for serving

## METHOD

**1.** Steam the crab for 8 minutes over vigorously boiling water. Remove the crab, let cool, then remove the top shell and clean. Cut the body in half and remove the legs and claws. Set aside.

**2.** Preheat a wok or large skillet, then heat the oil, add ginger and stir-fry until the ginger is fragrant (about 30 seconds).

**3.** Add the garlic and shallots with the crab pieces, and stir-fry for about 1 minute.

**4.** Combine the stock, sherry, oyster sauce, Worcestershire sauce, soy sauce and sugar, and pour into the wok. Cover and cook over medium heat for 3 minutes.

**5.** Remove the crab with tongs, and set aside on plate.

**6.** Add the dissolved cornstarch to the wok and cook, stirring, until the sauce thickens (about 1 minute).

**7.** Pour the sauce and shallot mixture onto a serving platter, reassemble the crab, and place the shell over the body to give the impression of a whole crab lying on the platter.

**8.** Trickle sesame oil over the surface, garnish with chili slivers, and serve with boiled rice on the side.

*Serves 4*

# Grilled Lobster With Lemon-Chervil Butter

## INGREDIENTS

14 cups/3.5L water
2 teaspoons/10mL salt
1–1$^1/_4$ lb/500–650g live lobsters
6 tablespoons/90mL butter, unsalted
4 tablespoons/60mL fresh lemon juice
8 sprigs chervil, leaves only, chopped
   (or substitute parsley)
1 teaspoon/5mL mixed herbs
1 lemon, quartered lengthwise

## METHOD

**1.** In an 8–10qt/7–9L stockpot over high heat, bring salted water to a rolling boil. Blanch the lobsters for 3 minutes. Immediately remove and chill in a large bowl filled with ice and water. In 2–3 minutes, when the lobsters have cooled enough to handle easily, place them on their backs on a cutting board. With a large, sharp kitchen knife or cleaver, cut each lobster lengthwise into two separate halves. Remove the intestinal tract from the tails, and rinse the halves under cold water to remove the tomalley (soft green liver). Crack each claw and remove the meat. Cut the claw meat into bite-size portions and place it in the split body cavity.

**2.** In a small saucepan, melt the butter slowly over a low heat, being careful not to let the butter brown. Add the lemon juice, chervil and mixed herbs. Stir to blend thoroughly and brush the mixture liberally onto the exposed meat of both lobster halves.

**3.** With the griller set on high, cook the lobster halves until the meat is opaque and nicely grilled (approximately 5 minutes). Serve immediately with fresh lemon wedges and remaining lemon chervil butter for dipping.

*Serves 4*

CRAB WITH GINGER

## Devilled Crab Bake

### INGREDIENTS

200g/7oz can crabmeat

1/4 cup/50g butter

2 onions, chopped

2 red bell peppers, chopped

2 stalks celery, sliced

3 cloves garlic, crushed

1/2 cup/125mL mayonnaise

1 tablespoon/15mL Worcestershire sauce

2 tablespoons/25mL fruit chutney

2 tablespoons/25mL chopped parsley

1/2 cup/125mL fresh white breadcrumbs

2 tablespoons/25mL butter, extra

1/4 teaspoon/1mL paprika

### METHOD

**1.** Drain and flake crabmeat. Melt the butter in a frying pan, add the onion, bell pepper, celery and garlic and stir over low heat until the vegetables are tender.

**2.** Stir in the crab, mayonnaise, Worcestershire sauce, chutney and parsley. Spoon into four 1 cup/250mL serving dishes.

**3.** Combine the breadcrumbs, melted butter and paprika, sprinkle over the crab mixture and bake at 400°F/200°C oven for 15 minutes or until golden brown and heated through.

*Serves 4*

## Crab Strudel

### INGREDIENTS

1/4 cup/50mL shallots, diced

2 cups/500mL mushrooms, sliced

1/4 cup/50mL onions, diced

1/4 cup/50mL melted butter

3lb/1.5kg lump crabmeat

2 teaspoons/10mL garlic, minced

1 teaspoon/5mL thyme

1 teaspoon/5mL oregano

salt and pepper, to taste

16oz/500g cream cheese

1/2 cup/125mL Parmesan cheese

1/4 cup/50mL heavy or whipping cream

6 sheets filo pastry

### METHOD

**1.** Sauté the shallots, mushrooms and onions in the butter. Add the crabmeat, garlic, herbs, seasoning and cheese. Cool down with the cream. Spoon into individual 1 cup/250mL casserole dishes and top with filo pastry. Brown in a preheated oven at 350°F/180°C for 7 1/2 minutes.

*Serves 5*

DEVILLED CRAB BAKE

# Sherried Crab Vol-au-Vents

## INGREDIENTS

3 cups/750mL mushrooms
3 tablespoons/45mL butter
2 tablespoons/25mL butter, extra
3 tablespoons/45mL all-purpose flour
1 cup/250mL chicken stock
1/2 cup/125mL cream
1lb/500g crabmeat, flaked
1/2 cup/125mL Parmesan cheese
1 1/2 cups/375mL baby spinach leaves
1/2 red bell pepper, finely diced
salt and cracked black peppercorns
2 tablespoons/25mL dry sherry
vol-au-vent cases

## METHOD

**1.** Sauté the mushrooms in 2 tablespoons/25mL of the butter, and set aside.

**2.** Melt the extra butter and stir in the flour. Cook, stirring, for 2 minutes.

**3.** Over low heat stir in the chicken stock and cream. When the sauce is boiling, add the crabmeat and mushrooms.

**4.** When the sauce comes to the second boil, add the Parmesan cheese, spinach and red bell pepper and season with salt and pepper.

**5.** Remove from the heat and add the sherry. Spoon into heated vol-au-vent cases.

*Serves 4–6*

# Crab-Stuffed Eggplant

## INGREDIENTS

3 whole eggplants, medium
2 medium onions, finely chopped
3 cloves garlic, finely chopped
1 stalk celery, finely chopped
2 bell peppers, chopped
1/2 cup/125mL butter
salt and pepper, to taste
1/2 lb/250g medium prawns (shrimp), peeled
1/2 lb/250g lump crabmeat
1/2 cup/125mL parsley, chopped
1 teaspoon/5mL paprika
1 cup/250mL breadcrumbs
2 teaspoons/10mL olive oil

## METHOD

**1.** Place the whole eggplants in large pot with enough water to cover them. Simmer until soft. Remove from heat and place in iced water. When cool cut the eggplants in half and scrape the flesh out. Be careful not to tear the skin. Next sauté onions, garlic, celery and bell peppers in butter until soft. Add the eggplant flesh that you scraped out and salt and pepper and cook until all the liquid has evaporated. Add the prawns (shrimp) and cook for about 5 minutes.

**2.** Turn the heat off and fold in the crabmeat, parsley, paprika and enough breadcrumbs to give the mixture a thick paste consistency. Fill the empty shells with the mixture and lightly spread the remaining breadcrumbs on top and sprinkle the olive oil on top of each half eggplant. Bake in a preheated oven at 350°F/180°C for about 25 minutes.

*Serves 6*

SHERRIED CRAB VOL-AU-VENTS

# Crab au Gratin

## INGREDIENTS

**4 small crabs**

**1 tablespoon/15mL chopped shallots**

**1/2 cup/125mL chopped mushrooms**

**1 tablespoon/15mL butter or margarine**

**2 tablespoons/25mL cognac**

**salt and pepper to taste**

*Gratin Sauce*

**2 tablespoons/25mL butter or margarine**

**2 tablespoons/25mL all-purpose flour**

**11/2 cups/375mL fish stock**

**1/2 cup/125mL light cream**

**1 teaspoon/5mL French mustard**

**1 teaspoon/5mL cayenne pepper**

**1/2 cup/125mL grated cheese**

## METHOD

**1.** Prepare the crabmeat in the usual way (see page 5) and set to one side, being careful to keep the shells intact. Sauté the shallots and mushrooms in the butter, season and pour the warmed ignited cognac over. Remove from the heat.

**2.** Make the sauce by melting the butter in a saucepan and stirring in the flour over a low heat for 1–2 minutes. Gradually add the fish stock and stir until the sauce thickens then stir in the cream, mustard and cayenne.

**3.** Allow to simmer for 2–3 minutes then remove from the heat and stir in the crabmeat and mushrooms. Spoon the mixture into the crab shells, sprinkle with cheese and bake at 330°F/165°C for 5 minutes.

*Serves 4*

# Grilled Lobster with Lemon-Lime Butter

## INGREDIENTS

**4 live lobsters (each 11/2 lb/750g)**

**1/2 cup/125mL salted butter**

**1/4 cup/50mL chopped cilantro**

**1 lemon, juiced**

**1 lime, juiced**

**lemon and lime wedges and cilantro sprigs, for garnish**

## METHOD

**1.** Bring a large pot of water to a rolling boil over high heat. Plunge the lobsters headfirst into the water and cook for 5 minutes, or until bright red. Remove the lobsters and plunge into a large bowl of cold water to stop the cooking.

Drain in a colander. Refrigerate if you do not plan to grill right away.

**2.** Prepare the lemon-lime butter. Melt the butter in a small saucepan over medium heat. Remove from the heat and stir in the cilantro and lemon and lime juice. Set aside.

**3.** Preheat the grill to high and brush with oil.

**4.** Place a lobster on its back on a cutting board. Using a large, sharp knife split the lobster down the middle, being careful not to cut completely through the shell. Remove the black vein from the tail, the tomalley (soft green liver) from the body and the sand sac located near the head. Repeat with the remaining lobsters. Baste the lobster meat

with some of the lemon-lime butter.

**5.** Grill the lobsters flesh-side down for 5–6 minutes, or until the flesh is just beginning to look opaque. Turn the lobsters over, baste with more lemon-lime butter and continue to cook for 4–5 minutes longer, or until the lobsters are cooked through. Transfer the lobsters to a large warm platter and garnish with lemon and lime wedges and cilantro sprigs. Transfer the remaining lemon-lime butter to a small dipping dish and serve separately.

*Serves 4*

# Lobster Sweet and Sour

## INGREDIENTS

*Court Bouillon*

2 cups/500mL dry white wine

2 carrots

2 celery stalks

1 onion

1 bouquet garni (see page 20)

1½ teaspoons/7mL coarse sea salt

black peppercorns

4 cups/1L water

1 lobster weighing 2¼lb/1kg

2 shallots

3 tablespoons/45mL butter

3 tablespoons/45mL olive oil

1 cup/250mL sparkling white wine

1lb/500g ripe tomatoes, blanched, peeled,
   seeded and chopped

salt and pepper, to season

1 teaspoon/5mL sugar

## METHOD

**1.** Make the Court Bouillon, in which to cook the lobster, with the white wine, the carrots, celery and onion cut in pieces, the bouquet garni, sea salt, a few peppercorns and the water. Prepare the lobster, add to the boiling court bouillon and cook gently for about 30 minutes. Drain well and, when slightly cooler, cut lengthwise down the middle. Remove the flesh carefully, reserving the shells.

**2.** Peel and finely chop the shallots and fry in the butter and oil. Add the sparkling wine and reduce by half. Add the tomatoes. Boil for 10 minutes, uncovered, to reduce and thicken, and season with salt and pepper. Add the sugar, simmer for 10 minutes more, then add the lobster flesh (still in 2 halves). Stir gently while cooking in the sauce for 5 minutes.

**3.** Remove the lobster halves from the sauce and replace the lobster in the half shells on a heated serving plate. Coat them with a little sauce and serve the rest on the side. Serve with a mixed salad.

*Serves 2*

# Surf and Turf

## INGREDIENTS

**2 porterhouse steaks**

**2 tablespoons/25mL butter**

**2 cloves garlic, finely chopped**

**1 large lobster tail**

**1 tablespoon/15mL chopped parsley**

## METHOD

**1.** Place the steaks on hot grill and cook to your liking. Remove to heated serving plates and keep warm.

**2.** Heat the butter in a frying pan and cook the garlic for 1–2 minutes. Carefully remove the shell from lobster tail and cut the flesh into pieces. Add the lobster and parsley to the pan and cook for 3–4 minutes over a medium high heat.

**3.** Spoon the lobster and butter over each steak and serve with grilled asparagus.

*Serves 2*

# Lobster Flambé

## INGREDIENTS

**2 lobsters weighing approximately**
   **1¹⁄₄lbs/625g each**
**3 tablespoons/45mL brandy**
**salt and freshly ground black pepper**
**butter, melted**

## METHOD

**1.** Rinse the lobsters under cold running water, dry with paper towels and cut lengthwise in half, using a strong, heavy kitchen knife.

**2.** Remove the sand sac in the head and the black thread running down the back (the intestinal tract). Season with salt and freshly ground pepper and generously brush all over the cut surface with melted butter.

**3.** Place on a very hot serving plate, heat 3 tablespoons/45mL of brandy, pour over the lobsters and set alight. Place on the table while still flaming.

*Serves 4*

# Lobster Bordelaise

## INGREDIENTS

**1 lobster weighing 2¹/₄ lbs/1kg**

**2 tablespoons/25mL olive oil**

**¹/₄ cup/50mL butter**

**¹/₄ cup/50mL good brandy**

**1 onion, finely chopped**

**1 carrot, finely chopped**

**1 small white celery heart, finely chopped**

**2 cloves garlic, crushed**

**2 shallots, finely chopped**

**1¹/₂ cups/375mL good red wine**

**2 tablespoons/25mL tomato paste**

**1 bouquet garni (see see page 20)**

**salt**

**freshly ground black pepper**

**few sprigs parsley, chopped**

**8 triangles white bread**

## METHOD

**1.** A live lobster is traditional for this dish. Use a cleaver or sharp, heavy kitchen knife to cut off the head and slice the body into steaks, cutting through the shell where the rings are jointed together. Remove and discard the black intestinal tract and the sand sac or stomach (found in the head). Crush the thin legs, collecting the juice which runs out and placing in a bowl, together with the liver. Reserve the coral if you have a hen (female) lobster.

**2.** Heat the oil in a large, deep pan with ¹/₂ of the butter, add the slices of lobster (still in the shell) and fry briskly until the shell is red. Transfer to a very hot flameproof dish, pour the heated brandy over, and flame.

**3.** Add the vegetables to the oil, butter and juices left in the pan and fry gently until tender. Pour in the wine, the juice from the lobster, the tomato paste, bouquet garni, salt and freshly ground pepper. Simmer for 15 minutes then discard the bouquet garni and liquidize the sauce. Return to the pan and add the lobster pieces. Cook gently for 10 minutes. If coral is present, measure out an equal amount of butter softened at room temperature and work the coral into it. Add 2 tablespoons/25mL of the sauce from the pan and mix well, then stir into the saucepan. Cook over the lowest possible heat for 10 minutes more.

**4.** Serve the lobster pieces coated with the sauce and sprinkled with parsley, surrounded by small triangles or shapes of bread toasted or lightly fried in butter.

*Serves 4*

# Fresh Crab Tagliatelle

## INGREDIENTS
3/4lb/375g dried tagliatelle

3 tablespoons/45mL olive oil

2 cloves garlic, chopped

1 red chili, de-seeded and chopped

finely grated rind of 1 lemon

2 fresh dressed crabs, to give

   about 3/4lb/375g crabmeat

1 cup/250mL light cream

1 tablespoon/15mL lemon juice

salt and black pepper

2 tablespoons/25mL chopped

   fresh parsley, to garnish

## METHOD
**1.** Cook the pasta until tender but still firm to the bite, then drain.

**2.** Meanwhile, heat the oil in a large heavy-based frying pan and gently fry the garlic, chili and lemon rind for 3–4 minutes, until softened but not browned. Add the crabmeat, cream and lemon juice and simmer for 1–2 minutes to heat through. Season to taste.

**3.** Transfer the pasta to serving bowls. Spoon the crab mixture over the top and sprinkle with the parsley to garnish.

*Serves 4*

# Grilled Rock Lobster

## INGREDIENTS
2 x 10oz/285g rock lobster tails, thawed

1 teaspoon/5mL salt

1 teaspoon/5mL paprika

1/8 teaspoon/1mL white pepper

1/8 teaspoon/1mL garlic powder

1/2 cup/125mL olive oil

1 tablespoon/15 mL lemon juice

## METHOD
**1.** Split the rock lobster tails lengthwise with a large knife.

**2.** To make the marinade, mix the seasoning with oil and lemon juice.

**3.** Brush the meat side of tail with the marinade.

**4.** Preheat a grill and place the rock lobster tails meat-side down and grill for 5–6 minutes until well scored.

**5.** Turn the rock lobster and cook for another 6 minutes, brushing often with the remaining marinade.

**6.** The lobster is done when it is opaque and firm to the touch.

*Serves 2*

FRESH CRAB TAGLIATELLE

# Lobster with Apples and Calvados

## INGREDIENTS

**3 apples**

**1 small carrot, chopped into small pieces**

**1 leek, cut into rings**

**1 small onion, coarsely chopped**

**6 cups/1.5L dry apple cider**

**salt and pepper**

**1 lobster weighing approx 2¹/₄lb/1kg**

**2 tablespoons/25mL sultanas or other
raisins, soaked in water**

**3 tablespoons/45mL heavy or whipping
cream**

**1¹/₂ tablespoons/20mL calvados (French
apple brandy)**

**¹/₄ cup/50mL unsalted butter**

**salt and pepper**

## METHOD

**1.** Use a firm variety of apple that will not disintegrate when cooked. Place the carrot, leek and onion in a deep, non-metallic saucepan. Remove the core from one apple but do not peel, cut into small pieces and add to the saucepan. Add all but ¹/₂ cup/125mL of the cider and season with salt and a little freshly ground white or black pepper.

**2.** Bring to the boil and boil for 2 minutes. If you are using a live lobster, add it to the fast boiling liquid now. Cover and cook for 10 minutes.

**3.** Peel, core and thinly slice the remaining apples and use to cover the bottom of a wide, shallow ovenproof dish. Sprinkle with the well drained sultanas. Spoon half the cream and the remaining cider over the apples. Place in the oven, preheated to 400°F/200°C, uncovered, for 10 minutes.

**4.** Drain the lobster. Boil the cider stock fast until reduced to about 2¹/₂ cups/625mL. Remove from the heat and when it has cooled a little, liquidize until smooth. Return the saucepan to the heat with the rest of the cream and the calvados and boil over a moderate heat until it has reduced further and thickened slightly. Remove from heat. Beat in the butter, a small piece at a time. Add salt and freshly ground pepper to taste.

**5.** If you have cooked the lobster in the cider, cut in half lengthwise at this point. If you have bought your lobster ready-cooked, place cut sides down on top of the apple slices for their last 5 minutes baking in the oven to warm through and take up a little of the apple and cider flavor. Remove and discard the small legs and antennae, the stomach sac, spongy gills and intestinal tract. Place each half on a heated plate, arrange the baked apple slices and sultanas on top and coat with the sauce.

*Serves 2 generously*

# Chili Crab

## INGREDIENTS

2 medium or 1 large crab

3 tablespoons/45mL vegetable oil

1 tablespoon/15mL lemon juice

salt

### Sauce

2–3 red chilies, seeded and chopped

1 onion, peeled and chopped

2 cloves garlic, peeled and chopped

2 teaspoons/10mL grated fresh ginger

2 tablespoons/25mL vegetable oil

2 ripe tomatoes, skinned, seeded and
   chopped, or 2 teaspoons/10mL tomato
   paste

1 teaspoon/5mL sugar

1 tablespoon/15mL light soy sauce

3 tablespoons/45mL water

## METHOD

**1.** Clean the crabs thoroughly, then cut each body into 2 or 4 pieces. Chop or crack the claws into 2 or 3 pieces if they are large. Heat the oil in a frying pan, add the crab pieces and fry for 5 minutes, stirring constantly. Add the lemon juice and salt to taste, remove from the heat and keep hot.

**2.** To make the sauce, put the chilies, onion, garlic and ginger in a blender and work to a smooth paste. Heat the oil in a wok or a deep frying pan. Add the spice paste and fry for 1 minute, stirring constantly. Add the tomatoes, sugar and soy sauce and stir-fry for 2 minutes, then stir in the water. Add salt if necessary and simmer for a further 1 minute. Add the crab and stir to coat each piece in the sauce and cook the crab through, only a minute or two. Serve hot.

*Serves 4*

Note: If using live crabs, the best way to handle them is to wrap them in paper and put in the freezer long enough to numb them. Then pierce and cut through eyes and shell, or with a heavy cleaver cut quickly in two.

# Lobster and Scallop Supreme

## INGREDIENTS

**2 cups/500mL rice**

**2¼lbs/1kg lobster**

**3 tablespoons/45mL butter or margarine**

**2 tablespoons/25mL lemon juice**

**1½lbs/750kg scallops**

**6 shallots, chopped**

**1 tablespoon/15mL chopped parsley**

## METHOD

**1.** Cook the rice in boiling salted water for 12–15 minutes. Drain and keep warm. Halve the lobster lengthwise and remove the digestive tract. Chop the flesh into bite-sized pieces.

**2.** Melt 1 tablespoon/15mL of the butter in a frying pan with the lemon juice and sauté the scallops and shallots until just tender. Add the lobster and allow to heat through.

**3.** Toss the parsley and remaining butter through the rice and spoon onto a heated serving plate. Spoon the seafood mixture into the shells and serve with the rice.

*Serves 4*

## Baked Crab and Prawns

### INGREDIENTS

1lb/500g crabmeat

1lb/500g prawns (shrimp), cooked

1/2 cup/125mL shallots, chopped

1/2 cup/125mL red bell pepper,
   chopped

3/4 cup/175mL celery, chopped

4 tablespoons/60mL lemon juice

3 tablespoons/45mL sweet chili sauce

1 cup/250mL mayonnaise

buttered breadcrumbs

### METHOD

1. Preheat the oven to 350°F/180°C.

2. Combine all the ingredients except breadcrumbs in a greased casserole dish. Top with buttered breadcrumbs.

3. Cook for 20–30 minutes, or until bubbly-hot.

*Serves 4–6*

## Lobster Alfredo

### INGREDIENTS

1 tablespoon/15mL butter

1/2 cup/125mL lobster fumet (fish stock)

2 cups/500mL heavy or whipping cream

2 cups/500g freshly grated Parmesan
   cheese

dash of Worcestershire sauce

1/4 teaspoon/1mL Tabasco sauce

1/4 teaspoon/1mL black pepper

1 teaspoon/5mL Dijon mustard

3/4 lb/375g fettuccine pasta

3/4 lb/375g fresh lobster meat

4 egg yolks

1/2 cup/125mL fresh chopped parsley

### METHOD

1. Over medium heat, in a medium-sized saucepan, melt the butter and add the lobster fumet and cream and turn the heat up to medium-high.

2. When the cream is hot, just before boiling, add the Parmesan cheese and whisk briskly until all the cheese is melted and dissolved into the cream.

3. Add the Worcestershire, Tabasco, black pepper and Dijon and whisk thoroughly again. Reduce the heat again to a fast simmer and allow the mixture to simmer for 20 minutes.

4. While the sauce is simmering, cook the pasta to your liking, drain and set onto plates. Cut the lobster meat into small pieces and add to the sauce. Add the egg yolks and turn the heat to medium-high. The sauce should be of medium thickness. Ladle the sauce over the pasta, sprinkle with the fresh chopped parsley and serve.

*Serves 4*

BAKED CRAB
& PRAWNS

## Sake-Simmered Lobster

### INGREDIENTS

**2 live lobsters, about 1 lb/500g each**

**2 leeks, cut into rounds**

**4 cups/1L watercress**

**3–4in/8–10cm fresh ginger**

**For Simmering**

**2 cups/500mL sake**

**1/2 cup/125mL water**

**7 tablespoons/105mL mirin**

**2 tablespoons/25mL dark soy sauce**

**2 tablespoons/25mL light soy sauce**

**2 tablespoons/25mL sugar**

**1/2 teaspoon/2mL salt**

**1 tablespoon/15mL fresh ginger juice**

**chervil leaves**

### METHOD

**1.** Cut the live lobsters in half lengthwise and then cut each half into 2–3 pieces.

**2.** Cut the leeks into 3/4in/2cm rounds, boil in salted water until just tender and drain.

**3.** Blanch the watercress in lightly salted boiling water, drain and refresh in cold water. Drain again and cut into 1 1/2in/4cm lengths.

**4.** Slice the ginger with the grain into very fine slivers and soak in cold water for 2–3 minutes.

**5.** Place the sake and water in a pan and bring to the boil over high heat, then add all the remaining simmering ingredients. Add the lobster and cover with a plate which fits down inside the pan and sits directly onto the food (this ensures even heat and flavor distribution by forcing the rising heat down). Boil for 5–6 minutes over high heat until the meat can be easily removed from the shell. Ladle the simmering liquid over the lobster several times. Add the leek and watercress. Heat through, add the ginger juice and immediately remove from the heat.

**6.** Divide the lobster and vegetables among 4 bowls. Pour in an ample amount of sauce. Top with well-drained ginger, garnish with chervil and serve.

*Serves 4*

SAKE-SIMMERED LOBSTER

# Lobster with Lemon and Dill Sauce

## INGREDIENTS

4 green lobster tails

$^1/_3$ cup/75mL butter

1 large clove garlic, crushed

$^1/_2$ cup/125mL sherry

2 tablespoons/25mL fresh dill, chopped

$^2/_3$ cup/150mL fish stock

$1^1/_3$ cups/325mL light cream

1 tablespoon/15mL tomato paste

salt, to taste

freshly ground black pepper

juice of $^1/_2$ lemon

1lb/500g spaghetti, boiled
   and drained

extra fresh dill, chopped

## METHOD

**1.** Remove the lobster meat from the shell and cut into medallions.

**2.** Melt the butter and sauté the garlic. Quickly add the lobster and sauté briskly. Set aside and keep warm.

**3.** Now add the sherry and dill to the pan and reduce the liquid by half. Add the fish stock, again reducing by half. Turn heat to medium and add the cream, tomato paste, salt and pepper and simmer for approximately 5 minutes.

**4.** Return the lobster meat to the pan together with its juices and add lemon juice to taste. Serve over hot pasta cooked al dente and garnish with the chopped dill.

*Serves 4*

# Green Mango and Lobster Curry

## INGREDIENTS

1¹/₂ cups/375mL coconut cream

1 teaspoon/5mL Thai green curry paste

1 stalk fresh lemon grass, bruised
   or ¹/₂ teaspoon/2mL dried lemon grass,
   soaked in hot water until soft

4 kaffir lime leaves, finely sliced

1 large green (unripe) mango,
   cut into ¹/₄in/5mm thick slices

1lb/500g lobster meat,
   cut into 2in/5cm cubes

1 tablespoon/15mL palm or brown sugar

2 tablespoons/25mL Thai fish
   sauce (nam pla)

1 tablespoon/15mL coconut vinegar

1 cup/500g cilantro, coarsely chopped

## METHOD

**1.** Place the coconut cream, curry paste, lemon grass and lime leaves in a saucepan and bring to the boil then reduce the heat and simmer for 5 minutes or until fragrant.

**2.** Add the mango and simmer for 3 minutes. Add the lobster, sugar and fish sauce and simmer for 7–8 minutes or until the lobster is cooked. Stir in the vinegar and cilantro.

*Serves 4*

# Lobster Lasagne

## INGREDIENTS

8 lasagne noodles, cooked and drained

1 onion, chopped

2 tablespoons/25mL butter

8oz/250g cream cheese, softened

1 egg, beaten

1 cup/250mL chopped dill pickles

2 teaspoons/10mL chopped basil

10fl oz/284mL can cream of
   mushroom soup

$1/2$ cup/125mL milk

$1/3$ cup/75mL white wine or chicken broth

$1/3$ cup/75mL seafood sauce

$3/4$lb/375mL can lobster meat, drained
   (several pieces of lobster meat can be
   set aside for a garnish, if desired)

10oz/285g scallops, thawed if frozen,
   cut in half

$2/3$ cup/150mL grated Parmesan cheese

2 cups/500g mozzarella cheese

## METHOD

**1.** Arrange 4 noodles to cover the bottom of an oiled 9in x 13in/23cm x 33cm baking dish. Sauté the onion in the butter just until tender. Stir in the cream cheese, egg, pickles and basil, mixing well. Spread half of this cheese mixture over the noodles.

**2.** Combine the soup, milk, wine, seafood sauce, lobster and scallops and fold over until well mixed. Spread half over the cheese mixture. Repeat layers with the remaining noodles, cheese and seafood mixture. Sprinkle with Parmesan cheese.

**3.** Bake uncovered at 350°F/180°C for 40 minutes or until heated through. Sprinkle with mozzarella cheese and bake for 2–3 minutes longer or until the cheese melts. Remove from the oven and let stand for 15 minutes before serving.

*Serves 10–12*

# Italian Lobster Pie

## INGREDIENTS

$1^1/2$ cups/375mL water

$1/4$ cup/50mL long-grain rice

8oz/250g skim milk ricotta cheese

2 eggs, beaten

2 cups/500g mozzarella cheese, chopped

$1/2$ lb/250g lobster meat, cut in small
   pieces

1 small onion, chopped

pinch black pepper

2 tablespoons/25mL Italian seasoned
   breadcrumbs

2 tablespoons/25mL milk

## METHOD

**1.** In a large saucepan bring water to a boil. Add rice and return to boiling, then reduce heat. Cover and simmer 20-25 minutes, or until done. Drain.

**2.** Stir in ricotta cheese, eggs, mozzarella cheese, lobster meat, onion and black pepper.

**3.** Butter a 12in/30cm quiche dish, coat with bread crumbs. Spoon lobster mixture into dish. Pour milk over mixture (this makes top brown and crusty after baking). Bake, uncovered, at 350°F/180°C for 45–50 minutes or until top is golden brown and knife inserted near center comes out clean.

*Serves 4*

# Grilled Creamy Lobster

## INGREDIENTS

3 medium cooked lobsters
3 tablespoons/45mL butter or margarine
1 small onion, chopped
3 tablespoons/45mL all-purpose flour
1 1/2 cups/375mL milk
3 tablespoons/45mL cherry liqueur
2 tablespoons/25mL grated mild
  Cheddar cheese
2 teaspoons/10mL French mustard
1/2 teaspoon/2mL English mustard
breadcrumbs
extra butter

## METHOD

**1.** Halve the lobsters lengthwise and remove the meat. Cut into chunks. Melt the butter and sauté the onion until tender. Add the flour and stir over a low heat for 2 minutes. Gradually add the milk and allow the sauce to thicken.

**2.** Add the liqueur and simmer for 2 minutes then stir in the cheese and mustards. Spoon a little of the sauce into the lobster shells, add the lobster and coat with the remaining sauce. Sprinkle with breadcrumbs and dot with butter. Grill until brown and bubbling. Serve immediately.

*Serves 6*

# Lobster Fradiavolo

## INGREDIENTS

2 x 1 1/2 lb/750g lobsters
4 tablespoons/60mL olive oil
2 teaspoons/10mL minced garlic
1/2 cup/125mL minced onion
2/3 cup/150mL minced celery
2/3 cup/150mL minced green bell pepper
2/3 cup/150mL chopped parsley
1/4 teaspoon/1mL black pepper
1 dash Tabasco sauce
1 dash Worcestershire sauce
1/2 teaspoon/2mL oregano
1/2 teaspoon/2mL basil
2 medium skinned, diced tomatoes
1/2 cup/125mL Marsala
1lb/500g cooked pasta
1/2 cup/125mL grated Parmesan cheese

## METHOD

**1.** Prepare the fresh lobster (see page 6) and then cook in boiling water. Remove from the water, lay the lobsters on their backs and cut them in half lengthwise with a chef's knife. Remove the intestinal tract that runs down the back of the tail section and the stomach. Save the tomalley (soft green liver) and the roe in a separate bowl to add later on.

**2.** In a large skillet, place the olive oil and garlic. Cook on high heat until the garlic starts to brown. Add the onion, celery, bell pepper, parsley, black pepper, Tabasco, Worcestershire, oregano and basil.

**3.** Cook over medium heat for 4–5 minutes then add the lobsters, split-side down. Pour the tomatoes, Marsala, tomalley (soft green liver) and roe over the lobsters, cover and cook on medium heat for 8–10 minutes. In a large shallow bowl, place 8oz/225g of the pasta. Remove the lobsters from the pan and place, the split-side up, on the pasta. Cover with the sauce, sprinkle with Parmesan cheese and serve.

*Serves 4*

GRILLED CREAMY
LOBSTER

# Stuffed Spiny Lobster

## INGREDIENTS

1 dried cloud-ear mushroom

2 live 1lb/500g spiny lobsters

4 fresh shiitake mushroom, washed
and stems removed, or 4 fresh brown
mushroom, washed and trimmed

1/4 medium carrot

2 stalks green asparagus, trimmed

7 tablespoons/105mL bonito stock (dashi)

1 tablespoon/15mL light soy sauce

1 tablespoon/15mL mirin

3 eggs, lightly beaten

## METHOD

**1.** Soak the cloud-ear mushroom for 1 hour. Cut the lobster in half lengthwise and remove the meat, reserving the shells. Cut the meat into 8 equal portions and drop in boiling water. When the surface of the meat whitens, immediately drain and plunge into iced water. Drain again and wipe dry.

**2.** Wash the shells thoroughly and boil in lightly salted water until they turn red.

**3.** Cut the shiitake (or brown) mushrooms into thin strips. Cut the cloud-ear mushrooms, carrot, and asparagus into 1$^1$/$_2$ in/4cm long slivers.

**4.** Preheat the oven to 440°F/220°C.

**5.** Combine the bonito stock and all the vegetables in a soup pot and bring to the boil over high heat. Season with soy sauce and mirin and boil for about 3 minutes until the vegetables are just tender. Pour in the beaten egg in a circular motion to cover, and stir gently.

**6.** Cover with a plate which fits down inside the pan and sits directly onto the food, and turn off the heat (this ensures even heat and flavor distribution by forcing the rising heat down). Let stand for 2–3 minutes and then drain.

**7.** Return the lobster to the shells. Top with the egg mixture and place in the preheated oven. When the surface of the egg mixture is lightly browned, remove the lobster from the oven, transfer to plates, and serve.

*Serves 4*

# Lobster à L'Américane

## INGREDIENTS

1 lobster, about 2lb/1kg
2 tablespoons/25mL olive oil
1/2 cup/125mL butter
1/2 cup/125mL brandy
6 shallots
1 cup/250mL dry white wine
1 cup/250mL fumet (fish stock)
4 fresh tomatoes, blanched, peeled, seeded
   and chopped (or canned)
1 sprig tarragon
1/4 cup/50mL butter, softened
1 tablespoon/15mL finely chopped parsley
salt and pepper

## METHOD

**1.** Buy a live lobster if possible and prepare it (see page 6). Chop into fairly large pieces, shell and all, collecting and reserving the juices. Discard the sand sac and remove the intestinal tract; reserve the greenish tomalley (soft green liver) and coral, if any.

**2.** Fry the lobster pieces briskly in olive oil, stirring in 2 tablespoons/25mL of the butter until their shell has turned bright orange-red. Drain off excess butter and pour in the brandy. Heat and flame.

**3.** Peel and finely chop the shallots and sweat in 3 tablespoons/45mL of the butter in a wide, fairly deep pan. Add the white wine and continue cooking until the wine has evaporated.

**4.** Add the lobster pieces, their reserved juice and the hot fish stock. Add the tomatoes and the sprig of tarragon. Simmer for 15 minutes. Work the coral into the softened butter. Remove the lobster pieces with a slotted spoon and place in a heated serving dish. Discard the tarragon.

**5.** Add the coral butter to the sauce in the pan, stir gently as the butter melts, and add the chopped parsley. Season to taste with salt and freshly ground pepper, pour over the lobster and serve at once.

*Serves 4*

# Lobster Thermidore

## INGREDIENTS

4 raw lobster tails
1 tablespoon/15mL butter
1 1/2 tablespoons/20mL all-purpose flour
1 cup/250mL milk
2 teaspoons/10mL German mustard
1 teaspoon/5mL wholegrain mustard
1/3 cup/75mL cream

*Crunchy Topping*

2 tablespoons/25mL Parmesan cheese,
   grated
1/3 cup/75mL dry breadcrumbs
1 tablespoon/15mL chopped chives
1/2 teaspoon/2mL lemon rind, grated
1 tablespoon/15mL butter, melted

## METHOD

**1.** Remove the flesh from the tails and chop into bite-sized pieces. Add the lobster shells to a large saucepan of boiling water, and cook for 1 minute (or until the shells change color). Drain shells, rinse under cold water and dry.

**2.** Melt the butter in saucepan, stir in the flour and stir over moderate heat for about 1 minute. Remove from the heat and gradually add the milk, stirring constantly. Return to heat and cook until the mixture boils and thickens.

**3.** Stir in the mustards and lobster flesh and cook over medium heat for about 2 minutes, or until lobster is cooked.

**4.** Remove from the heat, and stir in the cream. Spoon mixture into the lobster shells.

**9.** Mix all the topping ingredients in a bowl then sprinkle over the prepared lobster mixture. Place under griller for 5–8 minutes, until golden brown.

*Serves 4*

## Lobster in Mint Pesto

### INGREDIENTS

**Mint Pesto**

**1 bunch fresh mint**

**4 tablespoons/60mL almonds, toasted**

**1 clove garlic, crushed**

**1/4 cup/50mL lime juice**

**1/4 cup/50mL olive oil**

**2 uncooked lobster tails,**
   **halved lengthwise**

### METHOD

**1.** To make the pesto, place the mint leaves, almonds, garlic and lime juice in a food processor or blender and process to finely chop. With the machine running, slowly add the oil and make a smooth paste.

**2.** Preheat the oven to 400°F/200°C and place the lobster on a baking tray, spread the flesh with pesto and bake for 15–20 minutes or until the lobster is cooked.

*Serves 4*

Note: This dish is perfect for a special occasion meal. Start with an antipasto platter – purchase the ingredients from the delicatessen section of your supermarket. Accompany the lobster with boiled new potatoes tossed with olive oil and black pepper and a salad of assorted lettuces and chopped fresh herbs. Finish the meal with a good quality purchased ice cream topped with a spoonful of your favorite liqueur.

# Liz's Lobster

## INGREDIENTS

**4 small lobster tails**
**2 cups/500mL white wine**
**1/3 cup/75mL butter**
**2 tablespoons/25mL all-purpose flour**
**1/2 cup/125mL light cream**
**1 teaspoon/5mL lemon juice**
**1/2 teaspoon/2mL Dijon mustard**
**1 tablespoon/15mL capers, chopped**
**cooked rice to serve**

## METHOD

**1.** Simmer the lobster tails in the white wine until tender. Remove the lobster from the wine and set aside. Reduce the wine to 1/2 cup/125mL.

**2.** Melt the butter in a saucepan, add the flour and cook for 1 minute. Gradually add the reduced wine and stir until the sauce has thickened. Add all the remaining ingredients, except the rice, and stir until the sauce is simmering. Remove from the heat.

**3.** To serve, place the lobster tails on top of a bed of rice and top with the sauce. Garnish with fresh steamed asparagus.

*Serves 2*

# Lobster Quiche

## INGREDIENTS

6 well beaten eggs

3 cups/750mL sour cream

1/2 teaspoon/2mL Worcestershire sauce

1/4 teaspoon/1mL black pepper

1 teaspoon/5mL Dijon mustard

1 pie shell (see Savory Tart Pastry)

2 cups/500mL grated Swiss cheese

2 cups/500mL grated sharp Cheddar
   cheese

1/2 tablespoon/7mL chopped green onions

6oz/175g chopped lobster meat

paprika, for sprinkling

## METHOD

**1.** Preheat the oven to 375°F/190°C. In a medium-sized mixing bowl, blend the eggs, sour cream, Worcestershire, pepper and Dijon mustard together. (This is the quiche batter.) Arrange pastry in a pie shell. In a separate bowl, toss the two cheeses with the green onions and lobster. Place the lobster mixture into the pie shell. Add the quiche batter, sprinkle with paprika and bake until set and a knife inserted near center comes out clean (about 25–35 minutes). Let cool; serve at room temperature.

*Serves 4*

# Chinese Lobster Stir-Fry

## INGREDIENTS

1lb/500g lobster meat, fresh or frozen

1 small clove garlic, minced

2 tablespoons/25mL oil

1/2 cup/125mL chicken broth

1 small red bell pepper

2 cups/500mL bean sprouts

8oz/227mL canned or fresh water
   chestnuts

1 cup/250mL broccoli

1 cup/250mL Chinese cabbage, chopped

1/2 teaspoon/2mL salt

1/4 teaspoon/1mL pepper

1 egg, lightly beaten

## METHOD

**1.** If lobster is frozen, thaw. Chop into bite-sized pieces. In a skillet sauté the lobster and garlic in the oil for 1 minute. Add the broth and vegetables and simmer, uncovered, for 5 minutes. Season with salt and pepper.

**2.** Add a little of the hot broth to the beaten egg. Stir the egg mixture into the vegetables and lobster. Heat gently but do not boil. Serve with rice.

*Serves 4*

# Savory Tart Pastry

## INGREDIENTS

2 cups/500mL all-purpose flour

1/2 teaspoon/2mL salt

1/4 cup/50mL cold unsalted butter

2 egg yolks

4–6 tablespoons/60–90mL ice water

## METHOD

**1.** Sift flour and salt together onto work surface; make a well in the center.

**2** Place butter, yolks and 3 tablespoons/ 45mL of the water in the well. Using fingertips, pinch butter to mix with the water and yolks. With a dough scraper or pastry blender, gradually work flour into yolk mixture with a cutting motion to make coarse crumbs.

**3.** Gather crumbs into a rough mound. Work small portions of the dough against the work surface with the heel of your hand (pushing away from you), so that the dough is smeared across the work area surface. When pieces of dough are pliable and peel away from the surface in one piece, press into a ball. Wrap well and refrigerate until firm (about 2 hours).

CHINESE LOBSTER STIR-FRY

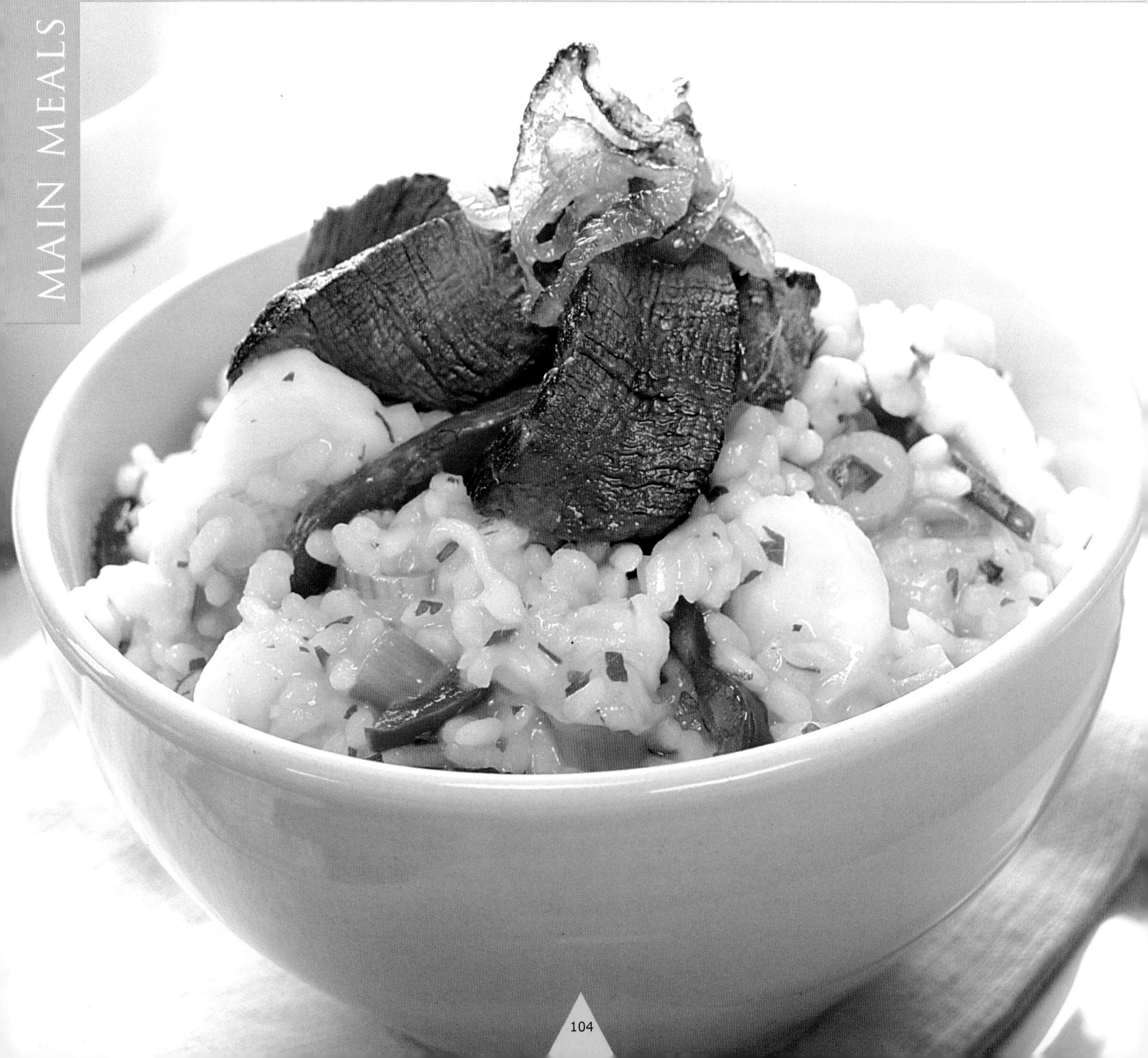

# Surf and Turf Risotto

## INGREDIENTS

2 onions, peeled and sliced

oil, for frying

2 tablespoons/25mL olive oil

4 cloves garlic

14oz/400g rib eye steak, cut into 2 pieces

10 green onions, chopped

1 red bell pepper, sliced into strips

2 cups/500mL arborio rice

$1/2$ cup/125mL white wine

4 cups/1L rich vegetable or
    chicken stock, simmering

2 lobster tails, cooked

1 tablespoon/15mL Parmesan cheese,
    grated

lots of fresh parsley, chopped

1 tablespoon/15mL sour cream

## METHOD

**1.** Peel and slice the onions. Either deep-fry at 350°F/180°C until crisp and golden, or toss with 2 tablespoons/25mL of olive oil and bake at 425°F/220°C for 30–40 minutes, tossing frequently, until golden. Set aside until the risotto is finished and ready to serve.

**2.** Heat the olive oil and gently fry the garlic for a moment or two. Add the beef and sauté until seared and crisp on both sides. Remove from the pan and keep warm, wrapped in foil. (For medium or well-done beef, bake at 400°F/200°C for 5 minutes or 10 minutes respectively, then keep warm wrapped in foil.)

**3.** To the oil and garlic mixture, add the green onions and bell pepper strips and sauté until softened.

**4.** Add the rice and stir to coat, then add the wine and simmer to evaporate the alcohol while the liquid is absorbed. When the rice mixture is firm, add the stock, half a cup/125mL at a time, stirring well after each addition and allowing each quantity of stock to be absorbed before the next addition. Continue in this fashion until the stock has all been incorporated. With the last addition of stock, add the lobster meat, cut into attractive, manageable pieces, and stir to distribute.

**5.** When almost all of the liquid has been absorbed and the rice is al dente, stir in the Parmesan cheese, parsley and sour cream.

**6.** Meanwhile, remove the warm meat from the foil and slice thinly. Serve the risotto in individual bowls, fan out the meat and place on top of the risotto. Garnish with the crispy fried (or baked) onions and serve immediately.

*Serves 4*

# King Island Lobster, Summer Herbs and Crustacean-Infused Olive Oil

## INGREDIENTS

**14oz/400g lobster**

**Court Bouillon (see page 75)**

*Lobster Tuilles*

**1 cup/250mL lobster stock**

**1/4 cup/50mL flour**

**1 1/2 tablespoons/20mL butter**

**salt and pepper to taste**

**dash of lemon juice**

**1 egg white**

**sesame seeds**

**salt and pepper**

**1 1/2 tablespoons/20mL olive oil**

**2 small potatoes, cooked and peeled**

**pinch of chervil, chives and tarragon**

**2 tomatoes**

**1/4 avocado**

**1/2 piece green mango**

**6 slices cucumber, skin removed**

**30g/1oz mixed seasonal lettuce**

**1/4 cup/50mL crustacean oil**

## METHOD

**1.** Immerse the lobster in boiling Court Bouillon for approximately 6 minutes. Drain and allow to cool, keeping the lobster $3/4$ cooked.

**2.** To make the Lobster Tuilles reduce the lobster stock to a syrupy consistency – approximately $1/3$ cup/75mL. Combine the flour and butter to form a paste. Mix in the reduction, salt, pepper, lemon juice and the egg white, a little at a time. Spread onto a greased tray as a sheet or pass through a stencil. Sprinkle with sesame seeds and bake at 350°F/180°C until golden brown (approximately 10 minutes).

**3.** Remove the meat from the shell keeping the tail intact; extract all the meat from the joints and legs. Slice the lobster tail into medallions and season with salt and pepper and a little olive oil. Finely dice the meat from the legs along with the end pieces of the tail. Lightly grill the lobster medallions. Slice the cooked potatoes, while still warm, into small rounds. Pinch the chervil and tarragon, chop the chives. Blanch, peel and de-seed tomatoes, reserve enough for 2 tomato rounds and dice the remaining along with the avocado. Add this to the chopped chives and chopped lobster and season.

**4.** Mound the mixture into the middle of the plate; garnish with strips of green mango, tomato and cucumber. Top with the grilled lobster medallions and potatoes. Dress the lettuce and place on top of the avocado mixture; sprinkle with the chervil and tarragon.

**5.** Drizzle the lobster slices with crustacean oil, garnish with Lobster Tuilles and serve.

*Serves 4*

SEAFOOD PIZZA

# Seafood Pizza

## INGREDIENTS

ready-to-use pizza crusts

pasta sauce

mushrooms

chopped mixed vegetables, to taste

grated cheese (combine Mozzarella,
   Cheddar and Monterey Jack)

variety of cooked seafood such as mussels,
   lobster meat, crabmeat, flaked fish,
   clams

## METHOD

**1.** Allow everyone to assemble their own pizzas.

**2.** Spread the crust with tomato sauce, add vegetables and seafood and top with cheese.

**3.** Be sure to have everyone place something different on the top of their own pizza so that you know whose is whose when it comes to the eating.

**4.** Place the pizzas on the top rack of an oven preheated to 400°F/200°C until the cheese melts and the pizzas are heated through.

*Serves a group*

# Crab-Stuffed Pasta Shells

## INGREDIENTS

1¹/₂lbs/750g crabmeat

1¹/₂lbs/750g cream cheese

1¹/₂ cups/375g grated Parmesan cheese

1 teaspoon/5mL minced garlic

¹/₂ cup/125mL chopped shallots

fresh ground pepper, to taste

¹/₃ cup/75mL chopped fresh tarragon
   or 1 tablespoon/15mL dried

¹/₂ teaspoon red bell pepper flakes

¹/₂lb/250g large pasta shells

4 cups/1L heavy or whipping cream

2 teaspoons/10mL minced garlic

2 tablespoons/25mL chopped shallots

salt and pepper, to taste

2 tomatoes, peeled, seeded and chopped

grated Parmesan cheese to garnish

## METHOD

**1.** Blend the first 9 ingredients and adjust the seasonings. Cook the pasta shells according to the instructions on the package. Prepare the cream sauce by combining the next 4 ingredients in a saucepan and heating until the mixture is reduced by half.

**2.** Pour the reduced cream sauce into a shallow baking dish that will hold the shells in one layer. Stuff the shells with the crabmeat mixture, arrange them on top of the sauce, and bake, covered, at 400°F/200°C for 15–20 minutes. Remove from the oven and top with the chopped tomato and Parmesan cheese.

*Serves 8–10*

# Lobster Cheese Casserole

### INGREDIENTS

1lb/500g lobster meat, diced
2 tablespoons/25mL butter
1/3 cup/75mL all-purpose flour
3/4 cup/175mL milk
1 1/2 cups/325mL whipping cream
1 cup/250mL Cheddar cheese, grated
1/2 teaspoon/2mL salt
1 green bell pepper, diced
1/2 cup/125mL Cheddar cheese, grated
pinch of paprika

### METHOD

1. Place the lobster in a greased 35oz/1L casserole dish. Over low heat, melt the butter, blend in the flour and slowly add the milk and cream. Cook, stirring constantly until the mixture is thick and smooth. Add the 1 cup/250mL cheese and the salt and green bell pepper. Stir until cheese melts. Pour over the lobster. Sprinkle remaining cheese over top and garnish with paprika.

2. Bake at 350°F/180°C for 15 minutes. Grill for 2 minutes to brown the top.

*Serves 4–6*

# Crab Supreme

### INGREDIENTS

1 cup/250mL butter
1 onion, chopped
1 green bell pepper, chopped
2 cups/500mL flour
2 teaspoons/10mL dry mustard
1/2 teaspoon/2mL salt
2 cups/500mL milk
2 cups/500mL grated Cheddar cheese
2 teaspoons/10mL Worcestershire sauce
28oz/796mL can tomatoes,
    drained and chopped
1lb/500g crabmeat (fresh or canned)

### METHOD

1. Melt the butter in a large saucepan. Sauté the onion and bell pepper in the butter until softened. Combine the flour, mustard and salt. Remove the pan from the heat and whisk in the flour mixture until smooth. Add the milk, stirring constantly, and return to the heat. Add cheese to pan. Cook, stirring constantly, on medium until the cheese has melted and the sauce is smooth and thick. Stir in the Worcestershire sauce. Add the tomatoes and crabmeat.

2. Pour into a casserole dish and bake at 400°F/200°C for 20 minutes until hot and bubbly. Serve over rice.

*Serves 6*

LOBSTER CHEESE CASSEROLE

## Lobster Mornay

### INGREDIENTS

**1 medium lobster, cooked and halved**

*Mornay Sauce*
**1¹/₃ cups/325mL milk**
**1 bay leaf**
**1 small onion, chopped**
**5 black peppercorns**
**2 tablespoons/25mL butter**
**2 tablespoons/25mL all-purpose flour**
**¹/₄ cup/50mL cream**
**²/₃ cup/150mL cheese, grated**
**salt and cracked black peppercorns**
**1 tablespoon/15mL butter, melted**
**1 cup/250mL fresh breadcrumbs**

### METHOD

**1.** Remove the lobster meat from the shells and cut into bite-sized pieces. Reserve the shells.

**2.** In a saucepan, place the milk, bay leaf, onion and peppercorns. Heat slowly to boiling point. Remove from the heat, cover and stand for 10 minutes. Strain.

**3.** In a pan, heat the 2 tablespoons/25mL butter, then remove from the heat. Stir in the flour and blend, gradually adding the strained milk. Return the pan to the heat, and stir constantly until the sauce boils and thickens. Simmer the sauce for 1 minute. Remove from the heat, add the cream, cheese, salt and pepper. Stir the sauce until the cheese melts, and add the lobster.

**4.** Divide the mixture between the shells. Melt remaining butter in a small pan, add the breadcrumbs, and stir to combine.

**5.** Scatter the crumbs over the lobster and brown under a hot grill.

*Serves 2*

## Lobster Creole

### INGREDIENTS

**2 tablespoons/30mL olive oil**
**¹/₂ slice medium red onion**
**¹/₂ slice medium green bell pepper**
**¹/₂ slice medium red bell pepper**
**¹/₂ slice medium tomato**
**¹/₂ teaspoon/2mL lobster base or fish stock powder**
**¹/₂ cup/125mL water**
**6oz/170g lobster tail and claw meat**
**¹/₂ teaspoon/2mL chopped garlic**
**1 tablespoon/15mL red hot sauce**
**1 teaspoon/5mL Cajun seasoning**
**2 tablespoons/25mL non-fat sour cream**

### METHOD

**1.** Heat the oil in a sauté pan to medium heat. Add the onion, bell peppers and tomato and sauté for 5 minutes. Add the lobster base or stock powder to water until dissolved. Transfer to the sauté pan. Add the lobster meat, garlic, red hot sauce and Cajun seasoning and simmer for 3 more minutes. Stir in the sour cream until desired consistency. Serve over white rice.

*Serves 1*

LOBSTER MORNAY

# Lobster Newburg

## INGREDIENTS

$^1/_4$ cup/50mL butter

$4^1/_2$lb/2kg lobster, boiled, shelled
   and cut into small pieces

2 teaspoons/10mL salt

$^1/_4$ teaspoon/1mL ground cayenne pepper

$^1/_4$ teaspoon/1mL ground nutmeg

1 cup/250mL heavy or whipping cream

4 egg yolks

2 tablespoons/25mL brandy

2 tablespoons/25mL dry sherry

reserved lobster tail shell or
   4–6 vol-au-vent cases

rice, for serving

## METHOD

**1.** In a shallow frying pan melt the butter over a moderate heat. When the foam subsides, add the lobster.

**2.** Cook slowly for about 5 minutes. Add the salt, cayenne pepper and nutmeg.

**3.** In a small bowl lightly beat the cream with the egg yolks. Add the mixture to the pan, stirring continuously.

**4.** Finally, add the brandy and sherry as the mass begins to thicken. Do not allow to boil or the sauce will curdle.

**5.** Serve either placed back in the lobster tail shell or in vol-au-vent cases. Serve with steamed rice.

*Serves 4–6*

GRILLED LOBSTER AND LEMON ANISETTE BUTTER

# Grilled Lobster and Lemon Anisette Butter

## INGREDIENTS

2/3 cup/150mL butter

juice 1 lemon

2 tablespoons/25mL Pernod

1 teaspoon/5mL dill or fennel seeds

3 large green lobster tails

## METHOD

**1.** Melt the butter in a saucepan and add the lemon juice, Pernod and dill. Stir well over medium heat and set to one side. Cut the lobster tails in half, remove the meat and cut into chunks then return the meat to the shell. Sit the tails on a grilling rack, brush liberally with the butter and place under the griller. Grill, brushing regularly with the butter until cooked. Serve with a tossed mixed lettuce and watercress salad.

*Serves 6*

# Louisiana Stuffed Crabs

## INGREDIENTS

1/2 cup/125mL margarine

1 onion, finely chopped

1 stalk celery, chopped

1/2 bell pepper, chopped

1lb/500g crabmeat

3 tablespoons/45mL minced green onion,
   bulbs only

2 tablespoons/25mL minced parsley

salt and pepper, to taste

2 teaspoons/10mL lemon juice

1 teaspoon/5mL Worcestershire sauce

1/2 teaspoon/2mL Tabasco sauce

1 egg beaten with 1/4 cup/50mL milk

6 cups/1.5L plain breadcrumbs

buttered breadcrumbs

## METHOD

**1.** Preheat the oven to 400°F/200°C. Melt the margarine in skillet over low heat. Add the onion, celery and bell pepper and cook slowly until tender. Add the crabmeat, green onion, and parsley and simmer for about 10 minutes. Add the salt, pepper, lemon juice, Worcestershire sauce, Tabasco and egg-milk mixture.

**2.** Set aside to cool slightly. Add the plain breadcrumbs to obtain stuffing consistency. Stuff the crab shells and top with the buttered breadcrumbs. Bake for 15 minutes, or until lightly browned.

*Serves 8*

LOBSTER PROVENÇALE

# Lobster Provençale

## INGREDIENTS

1/4 cup/50mL butter

1 teaspoon/5mL freshly crushed garlic

2 green onions, chopped

14oz/398mL can tomatoes

salt and cracked black peppercorns
  (to taste)

pinch of saffron

1 large cooked lobster

1/4 cup/50mL brandy

boiled rice

1/2 bunch fresh chives, chopped,
  for garnish

lemon wedges, for garnish

## METHOD

**1.** In a shallow frying pan, melt the butter over a moderate heat. Add the garlic, green onions, tomatoes, salt and pepper and saffron. Cook until the onions are translucent (about 2 minutes).

**2.** Remove the meat from the lobster, and cut into large pieces. Add the lobster to the frying pan and flame with the brandy. Cook gently until the lobster is heated through.

**3.** Place the rice on a serving plate and sprinkle with chives.

**4.** Remove the lobster from the frying pan, retaining the cooking liquid as a sauce.

**5.** Arrange the lobster on the rice and spoon the sauce (which has been cooked with the lobster) over the lobster. Serve with the lemon wedges on the side of the plate.

*Serves 4*

# Lobster Forestiere

## INGREDIENTS

2 x 1lb/500g fresh lobsters

1 cup/250mL light cream

4 tablespoons/60mL butter

1/4 cup/50mL finely chopped shallots

3 cups/750mL chopped mushrooms

1 tablespoon/15mL all-purpose flour

2 teaspoons/10mL Dijon mustard

1 teaspoon/5mL Worcestershire sauce

2 egg yolks

Tabasco sauce, salt and pepper, to taste

1 cup/250mL buttered breadcrumbs

2 tablespoons/25mL finely chopped
  parsley

## METHOD

**1.** Steam the lobster in 3/4in/2cm of water for 10 minutes. Strain and reserve 1/4 cup/50mL of liquid.

**2.** Warm the cream in a small saucepan. Melt the butter in another saucepan and sauté the shallots and mushrooms until tender. Stir in the flour and cook until bubbling. Remove from the heat and whisk in the warm cream. Return to the heat and boil, stirring constantly, until the sauce thickens. Simmer for at least 3 minutes. Add the mustard and Worcestershire sauce.

**3.** Whisk the egg yolks and lobster liquid in a bowl. Whisk in 1/2 cup/125mL of the hot sauce, a spoonful at a time. Slowly beat in the remaining sauce. Add the Tabasco and season to taste. Transfer the enriched sauce to the saucepan and, stirring carefully, bring to a simmer over moderate heat.

**4.** Arrange the lobsters in their shells on a baking sheet. Distribute the creamed mushroom sauce over the lobsters. Top with a mixture of buttered crumbs and parsley. Bake at 450ºF/230ºC for at least 5 minutes until the breadcrumbs begin to brown.

*Serves 4*

# Crab Tempura

## INGREDIENTS

**6 large crab legs**

**all-purpose flour**

**1 cup/250mL tempura batter (see below)**

**1 sheet nori seaweed, cut into**
**  2in/5cm strips**

**lemon wedges**

## METHOD

**1.** Carefully break the shell away from the thick end of each crab leg. Leave the thin end of the leg still covered with shell.

**2.** Make the tempura batter as described below. Dust the crabmeat lightly with flour. Dip the meat end of the crab stick into the tempura batter. Deep-fry the whole leg at 350°F/180°C until the batter is crisp and golden.

**3.** Gently tie each of the seaweed strips into a knot, dip into the tempura batter and deep-fry until crispy.

**4.** Arrange the crab on a large serving plate and garnish with lemon wedges and fried seaweed.

### *Tempura Batter*

Place 1 egg yolk and 1 cup/250mL of iced water into a bowl and mix together. Add 1$\frac{1}{2}$cups/ 375mL of all-purpose flour or tempura flour and mix roughly with chopsticks or a fork. Do not over-mix, the mixture should be lumpy. Use immediately while batter is still cold.

*Serves 3*

# INDEX

# INDEX

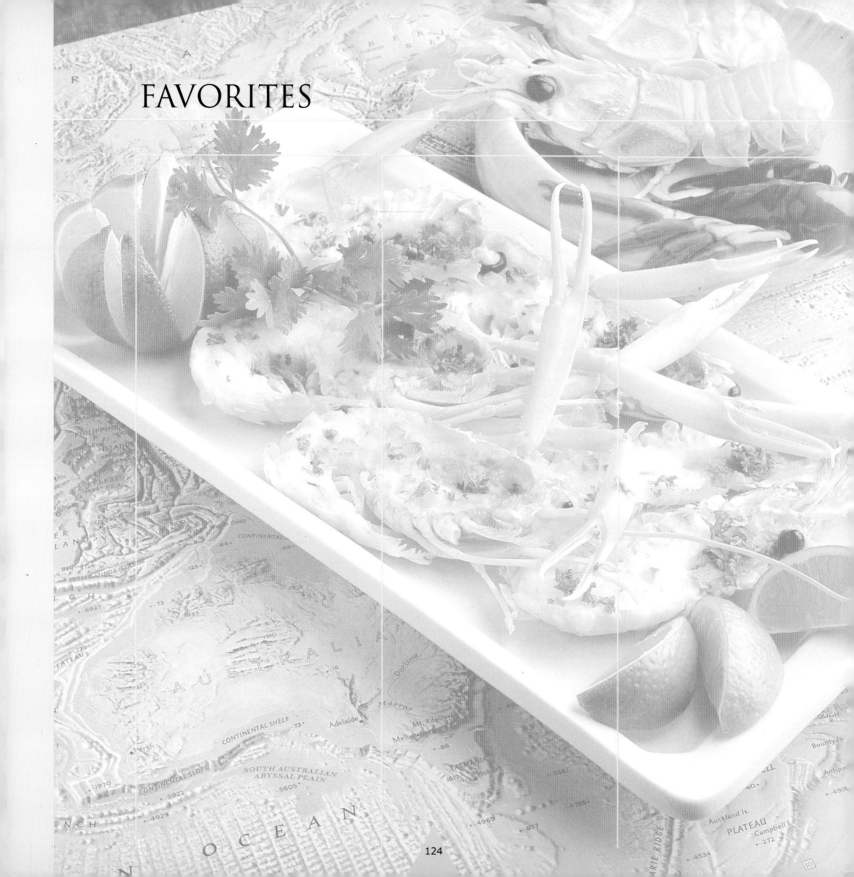

# FAVORITES

# FAVORITES

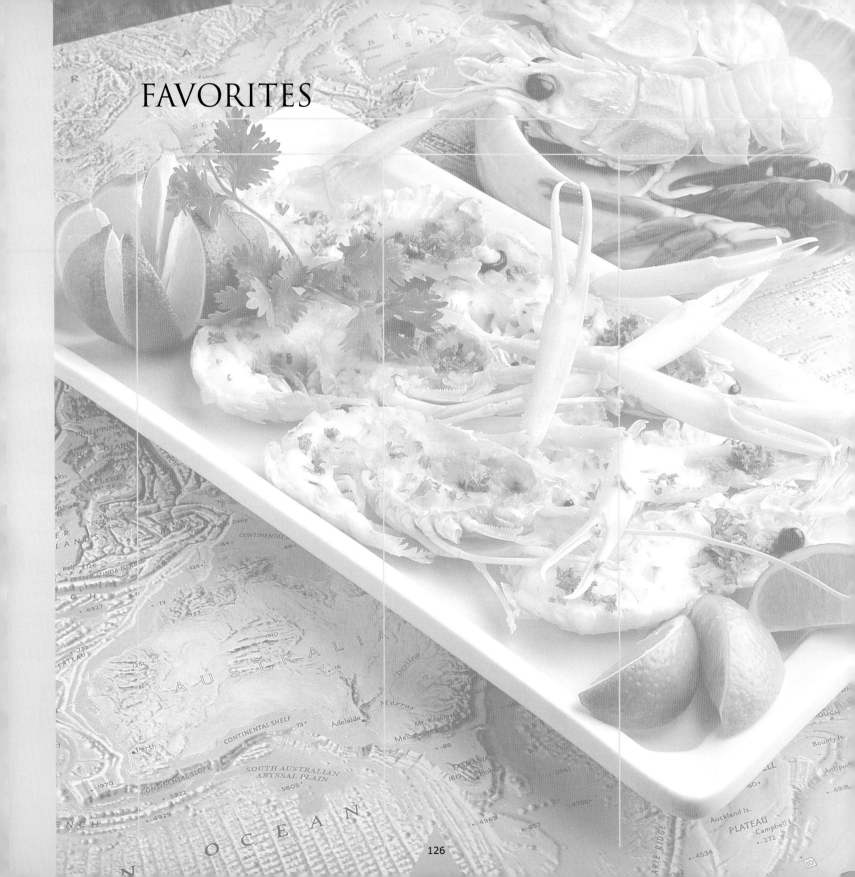

# FAVORITES

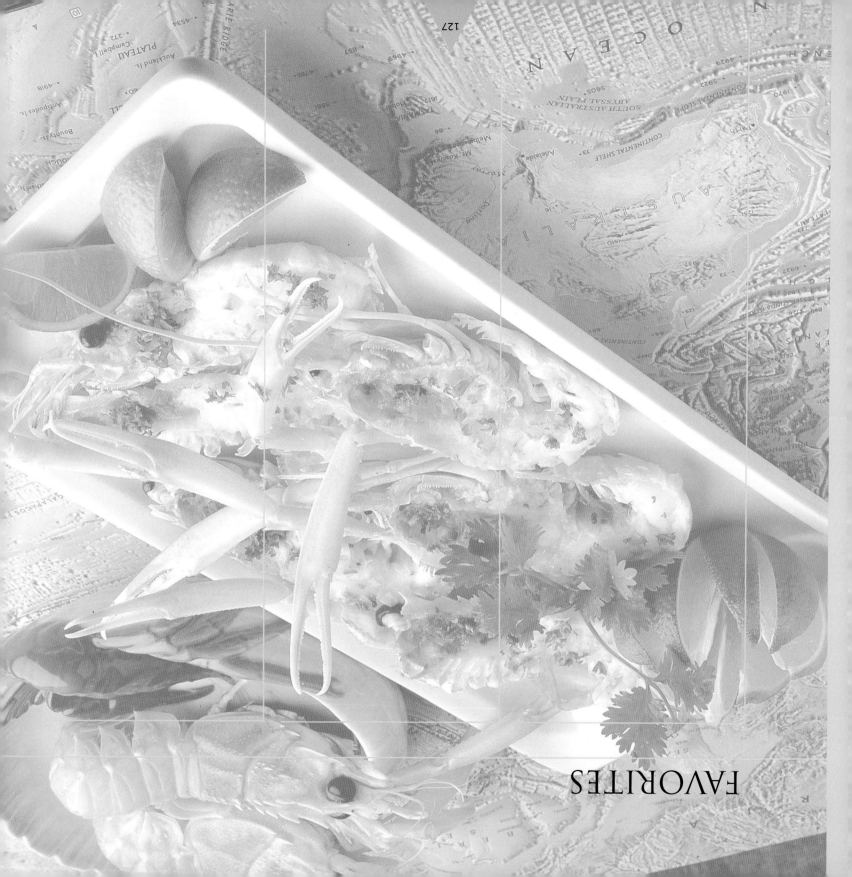

FAVORITES

FAVORITES